In Search of Gold

A Memoir of One of New York City's Finest

by Gary M. Rosen
as told to Dean Palamara

Art Direction & Graphic Design
by Dawn Arrington, Ad Pizazzz
www.AdPizazzz.com

Volossal
Publishing

Published by Volossal Publishing
www.volossal.com

Copyright © 2021
ISBN 979-8-9850796-2-3

Table of Contents

I dedicate this book to both my wife and daughter. My marriage to Christine over the many years has become very strained. I am not the same person that she married. She deserves better. My relationship with my daughter Jodi Michelle, remains strong. I tried my best to be a good father. Because I was not able to celebrate holidays, family and school functions like other fathers, I missed a big part of her childhood. The job always came first. I can't say my father didn't warn me that this would happen. May God always bless them.

- Gary Rosen

To my mother, Mattie, a prodigious reader, who endearingly introduced me to the wonderful world of the written word.

- Dean Palamara

June 11, 1982

I stopped the unmarked car directly behind the vehicle that was parked in the dark on the right side of the road. As I hit my headlights' high beams, they shined through the other car's rear window and out through its windshield, indicating an empty automobile. So I pulled alongside the parked car with my partner, Detective Fahey, in the passenger seat.

A man jumped up and came out of the other vehicle, shouting, "What the fuck you doin'?"

Suddenly, our passenger side window exploded. I turned to see blood shooting out from between Bobby Fahey's fingers as he held his face.

"I'm shot, Gary!" he cried, leaning forward.

Bobby somehow managed to stick his right arm out the opening where the window had been and fired a shot.

I swung out of the driver's door with my 6-shot Colt Detective Special revolver in my hand and moved quickly around the back of the car. The assailant was upon me before I could clearly see him, attacking me with a club-like weapon. This guy, about 6' 2" and 220 pounds, towered over my 5' 11", 165 pound frame. With my free hand I grabbed the guy by the arm that held the club and brought the full force of my handgun down on his head with my other hand. As he fell, I could see that he was wearing a red shirt but was otherwise naked.

The son-of-a-bitch actually got up and came at me again. I didn't realize then that he'd already taken a bullet through his heart, lung and liver.

I clocked him a second time, knocking him down. Unbelievably, he arose to come at me once more. This time my blow to his head felled him hard. He was never to get up again.

I called in a 10-13: Officer Down. I requested an ambulance to Goethals Road North which was a service road for the Staten Island Expressway.

A woman came out of the parked car's passenger side, shouting in my direction. She was nude and covering the front of her body with articles of clothing she was holding.

"Get back in the car," I told her.

A patrol car arrived before the ambulance, so I put Bobby in the patrol car and had the responding officers take him to the hospital.

Final closure on this case took years to reach.

Introduction

Irish-Americans have traditionally predominated as members of the New York City Police Department. This is the true story of a Jewish-American boy living in the city's projects, whose dream was to earn the Gold Shield of a New York City Police Detective and follow in the footsteps of his father. No names have been changed to protect the innocent – or the guilty.

America in the 1960's and 1970's was a tumultuous time of cultural clashes, political intrigue and the development of contemporary criminal organizations. The case overload for detectives during this time was extreme, challenging the entire New York City Police Force. One very young cop relished his role in pursuing justice and accumulated a diverse resume of successful investigations for which he received well-earned recognition.

Many people believed that the two most prestigious positions in the New York City Police Department were Chief of Detectives and Gold Shield Detectives. These two ranks held a certain mystique in the eye of the public. To attain a Civil Service rank, like Sergeant, Lieutenant or Captain, an applicant was required to pass an exam, and would then be assigned to perform uniformed duty at the new position for a period of two years or more. Higher ranks were political appointments. Some aspiring members of the Police Force preferred plain clothes duty, and opted not to return to wearing the uniform.

Gold Shield Detective was a prized rank, because to be awarded such a distinction one achieved it strictly through the merits of his performance.

Part One
Rookie

Russell Rosen
NYPD 1953 - 1975

Chapter One

My father, Russell Rosen, became a New York City Police Patrolman in June of 1953 when he was officially sworn in. While he was at the old Police Academy on Hubert Street in Brooklyn, he wore a gray uniform. His first assignment as a patrolman in uniform, now in blue, was with the 63rd Precinct in Flatbush, Brooklyn.

During the summer months, Coney Island was a hub of activity, requiring a larger police presence to oversee the season's influx of people and activity. For these summer details, Dad was assigned to the 60th Precinct on Coney Island, where one of my earliest (and most humorous) memories of his work took place. He'd take our family to join him at the Washington Baths, where there were tennis courts, a salt water swimming pool and other activities. My father played handball often and participated in the handball tournaments there, for which Washington Baths was noted.

Men would gather by the dozens in the men's locker room to gamble at cards and dice, a favorite of my father's. One day when I was very young, perhaps 6 or 7 years old, my father was shooting dice with a large group of men when an unannounced police raid hit. Uniformed cops swarmed the locker room, gathering the gamblers, my Dad included. They knew that he was on the job, so the arresting officers asked him how he wanted to handle this situation. My Dad went back to our cabana, took out a smoking jacket, put it on, and pinned his badge on the smoking jacket. He then returned to the locker room and helped the uniformed officers arrest the others, his fellow gamblers. A memorable sight!

Time with my father at Coney Island was exciting for a youngster. He'd flash his badge at rides and we'd go on for free. Sometimes we'd go to the movies together, again for no charge when they saw that he was a cop. In those days, most policemen only made perhaps $3,000 – $3,500 per year, so these perks were considered commonplace.

Following his tour with the 63rd, Russell Rosen worked for the Youth Squad out of the 71st Precinct, on the corner of Empire Boulevard and New York Avenue in Brooklyn. He then became a Detective and was assigned to the 64th Detective Squad in Bay Ridge, Brooklyn.

Gary Rosen
NYPD 1968 - 1985

Chapter Two

In 1966 I took the test for the New York City Police Department and passed. In 1968, just after being sworn in as a Trainee, I attended the Police Academy. At the ceremony I was sworn in by Louis Stutman, the Chief Clerk. He was the highest ranking civilian officer in the New York City Police Department at that time, and became Executive Secretary to Police Commissioner Kennedy, and later the first Chairman of the Civilian Complaint Review Board. Stutman was also a prominent member of the Shomrim Society. We accomplished all the training and took all the tests that police officers did, except for firearms training, which I received at a later date. Those of us under the age of 21 were not authorized to carry firearms.

My father made it clear at that time that he was against my wanting to become a cop. He and my mother were divorced in 1962, and the job he worked was assuredly a contributing factor. The divorce rate for cops was as high as 50%. Later, he would again express his displeasure with and concern for my career decisions more vehemently, but once I got going he became proud of me.

New York City Police Department trainees were assigned various duties, including those in the Bureau of Criminal Identification (BCI) – fingerprint classification and arrest records; the Information Unit; and the Communications Bureau. Some trainees were immediately assigned to precincts as switchboard operators, and others were weeded out of police work, found unfit due to overall sloppiness, lack of pride in their duties, or were outright fired for drug use.

Upon completion of the recruit training at the Police Academy, I was included in a group of graduates who were sent for specialized training for reading fingerprints (dactylograms) under the BCI. These courses were held at the Academy. All arrest fingerprints went to the BCI, and at that time prints were the only way of positively identifying a suspect from a crime scene. There was no DNA available at that time, so the use of fingerprints were relied on heavily in the criminal justice system. Because every individual had different prints, this became conclusive identifying evidence. Witnesses were asked to identify suspects from either a line-up or from mug shot photos, but often witnesses were unable (or reluctant) to make positive identification from this method. Many times at the scene of a crime, the area would be dusted in a search for "latent" prints which would be lifted using a special tape, then transferred onto a correspondingly special card. These prints would be sent to the "Latent Prints" section of BCI for clarification, in the hopes of making a match with prints already on file.

The instructors for this fingerprint training were two detectives. One was Arthur Addis, whose son later came on the job with the NYPD. The other was the top fingerprint man in the U.S., Bill Manning, who had been called to match Lee Harvey Oswald's fingerprints to the rifle used to shoot President John Fitzgerald Kennedy.

There were two groups for fingerprint recordkeeping. A: Prints of all policemen and individuals filing for licenses. B: (Classified) Prints of those arrested for crimes (criminal prints). The criminal individuals with these prints would be issued a "B" number, which would follow them forever. There were "B" folders which included a person's "yellow sheet", or arrest record and fingerprint classification. A yellow sheet would always remain in a person's folder and a record of subsequent crimes by that individual would be added to those already listed on that person's yellow sheet. These folders were kept in the "B Cage". There were also index cards with criminal's names and particulars, such as fingerprint classification.

Long before my time (the 1950's and early 1960's), the people who'd worked in this special department were referred to as "90 Day Wonders". This came about because those who'd worked there for more than 90 days were given a Gold Shield, as the Department wanted Gold Shield Detectives to testify in court. My experience with the Bureau of Criminal Identification early on in my police career held me in good stead throughout my police work.

Upon the completion of the fingerprint course, I was assigned to BCI at 400 Broome Street, Manhattan, across from Police Headquarters.

Living in Queens, I traveled to work in Manhattan by bus, subway, car or motorcycle. In April of 1969 I was riding my motorcycle on the way to the BCI office for an 8-4 shift from home in Howard Beach, Queens, which was in the confines of the 106th Precinct, when I was struck by car at Woodhaven Blvd and Union Turnpike.

I sustained severe injuries, and was semiconscious. A patrol car arrived, found my police ID and the arriving radio car operators made a decision to not wait for an ambulance to arrive. They put me in their patrol car and took me to Jamaica Hospital, where I was in the ICU for 10 days. About a week later, I was discharged from the hospital and began rehab, including physical therapy (P.T.). At this time, the Department assigned me to light duty at my resident Precinct, the 106th, so I wouldn't need to commute to Manhattan.

I did not return to BCI until April, 1971.

The building in which the 106th Precinct operated was no architectural work of art. Located in Ozone Park, Queens and shrouded in a veil of grimy New York soot, the entire neighborhood at night was dark and foreboding.

~

My name is Gary Rosen. As a twenty-year-old trainee, I was assigned to the switchboard at the precinct station house during the overnight shift (0001 – 0800 – midnight until 8 o'clock in the morning) taking incoming calls. The desk officer I was assigned to held the rank of Lieutenant. I followed his duty chart: 4 days on – 56 hours off; thus the shift rotated 8 hours at each change. Patrolmen and their respective Sergeants worked off a different duty chart: 5 days, with a range of 48-72 hours off, also with rotating shifts.

Whoever was at the switchboard handled the incoming calls from anyone, paying particular attention to communication between radio cars and foot patrols during the midnight shift. Generally, the switchboard received such calls on an hourly basis, from both foot patrolmen and those in radio cars, to coordinate the safety of all personnel in the confines of the 106th Precinct. Sector cars and foot patrolmen made these "rings" to the precinct from call boxes in their sector. These were dangerous times, when numerous police shootings occurred, so the well-being of patrolmen was paramount. If any officers weren't heard from as expected, a search for them would be made.

During this time New York City Police patrol cars were green, black and white. As the department began converting to blue and white cars, they started painting numbers atop the patrol cars' roofs, so that they could be identified from the air by helicopters, using searchlights during the dark hours. The helicopters in the Aviation Unit were housed at the Floyd Bennett Field of the U.S. Navy Air Base on Flatbush Avenue in Brooklyn.

On the night of June 4, 1970, I received a telephone call at the switchboard and was sufficiently intrigued by the caller to take action. The unknown male voice inquired about any police knowledge of a grievous Assault & Robbery of a Bar and Grill located on Metropolitan Avenue, in Queens. Sensing the caller's possible complicity with the case, I was able to prolong the conversation long enough to elicit the caller's name and location. Telling the caller I'd consult the precinct's records, I asked that he telephone me back in thirty minutes for his information request.

My previous BCI experience suggested I use that time to call the Criminal Identification Bureau, where I learned that the caller's name was a match for an individual with a long previous criminal record – 9 prior arrests, and that he had served 2 years at Sing Sing and was currently wanted for Violation of Parole. I first reported to the 106th desk officer, Lieutenant Brendan King. Then I went upstairs to the 106th Detective Squad and gave a brief report to Detective Daly. He, in turn, met with Detective Roman of the 104th Precinct (where the call had come from) and they were jointly dispatched to the location the caller had given, just before I received the awaited return call. The detectives got there while the same caller was again in telephone conversation with me, still talking and oblivious to their arrival.

Following an investigation, Bernard Kissane (Male, White, 43) was arrested and charged with Robbery 1st degree and Possession of a Dangerous Weapon (.22 caliber Pistol). The owner of the Bar and Grill, Thomas Schultz, was the complaining witness. The Arresting Officer was Detective Roman of the 104th Squad.

To me, though pleased to learn of the arrest, this was another day's work. However, on August 29th the Commanding Officer at the 106th Detective Squad, Lieutenant Stanley A. Cafaro wrote to the Chief of Personnel. The subject: "Exceptional Police Work Performed by Trainee," noting the events of that shift of mine on June 4, 1970, when I assisted members of the 104th and 106th Detective Squads. The Lieutenant's letter noted my "Rosen I.D. #60834. 106th Precinct." Each precinct had a Commanding Officer who was responsible for the overall precinct and all the uniformed personnel serving there. In addition, there was a separate Commanding Officer for each Detective Squad.

On May 4, 1971 in an Official Police Department letter that Wilfred H. Horne, Deputy Commissioner, Press Relations wrote to me, he requested my presence on June 7, 1971 at Police Headquarters, 240 Centre Street at 11am, where I was to receive a Police Department Civilian Commendation Bar, together with a Certificate of Commendation "for your heroic and unselfish act on June 4, 1970, when you assisted members of the 106th Detective Squad in arresting a felon," presented by Police Commissioner Patrick V. Murphy. Thus, I earned unexpected recognition that early morning, early in my career.

These so-called "heroic" efforts of mine were widely published in articles at that time. The Long Island Press (Thursday, September 3, 1970) Sets Trap/Cop Trainee Cited ; The Brooklyn Spectator (Friday, September 11, 1970) Future Sleuth Follows In His Dad's Footsteps; The Chief – The Civil Employee's Weekly (Wednesday, June 14, 1971) Bravery Brings Honors/Civilians Risk

Life And Limb In Going To Aid Of The Police; and Civil Service Leader- America's Largest Weekly for Public Employees (Tuesday, June 15, 1971 Police Honor 5 CS Workers and Ten Civilians).

In a subsequent letter, written by the Commanding Officer of the 106th Precinct, Captain William McGarry to the Police Commissioner on September 8th, requesting a "Departmental Recognition: Police Trainee Gary Rosen, assigned to the 106th Precinct, on June 4, 1970, by clever and alert thinking, supplied information that led to the arrest of one male for Robbery, 1st Degree and possession of a dangerous weapon."

The Shomrim Society is a Brotherhood of those in the New York City Police Department of Jewish faith. In the Shomrim Newsletter of February, 1969 I was admitted to their organization, thanks to my father, Brother Russell Rosen and Shomrim President David Frischer, who'd introduced an amendment to their constitution and by-laws, making Police Department Trainees eligible. Detective Rosen was proud of his son's admittance, and I became active in the society, receiving letters of thanks for my work with them on Passover Charity Distribution in 1971 and 1972, and periodically for later work with the society.

I was a slim, impressionable young kid at the time and I was excited to be a part of police work.

On July 26, 1971, by Special Orders No. 129 by the Office of the Police Commissioner, I was officially appointed to the position of Patrolman in the Police Department of the City of New York, "having reached the age of twenty-one years [D.O.B. 7-5-50] and having passed the medical examination."

Shield No. 13112 was assigned to me. My career as a cop became official.

August 29, 1970

From: Commanding Officer, 106 Squad

To: Chief of Personnel

Subject: EXCEPTIONAL POLICE WORK PERFORMED BY TRAINEE.

    1.   On June 4, 1970, while performing tour 0001 to 0800 hours, police trainee, Gary M. Rosen, was performing telephone switchboard duty, when he received an incoming call from an unknown male who inquired about any police knowledge of a previous Assault & Robbery of a Bar & Grill located on Metropolitan Avenue, in Queens.

    2.   During telephone conversation, Trainee Rosen sensed caller's possible complicity with case and kept caller in conversation until he finally elicited caller's name and location. Trainee Rosen then asked caller to call back in one half hour during which time he would consult precinct records for caller's information request.

    3.   Having had previous BCI experience, Trainee Rosen called said unit for a name check of caller and received the information that caller possessed a long criminal sheet. Trainee Rosen then notified desk officer, Lieutenant Brendan King, and Detective third grade, John Daly, shield # 848, 106 Squad, forwarding at the same time all of the acquired information.

    4.   Detective Daly and Detective George Roman, shield # 2129, 104 Squad, proceeded to 34-06 Jordan Street, Flushing, Queens, where subject was located still on the telephone in conversation with Trainee Rosen. Subject was questioned and placed under arrest for possession of a .22 calibre pistol. Subsequent investigation revealed subject was perpetrator of a previous Assault & Robbery of a Bar & Grill located at 79-56 Metropolitan Avenue, Queens, U.F. 61 # 2944, 104 Precinct, on June 3, 1970.

    5.   Person arrested was identified as Bernard Kissane, M-W-43, name given to Trainee Rosen by caller, B# 334 003, of 34-06 Jordan Street, Queens. Criminal record indicates nine (9) previous arrests including arrests for A&R, Grand Larceny & Forgery, Felonious Assault, and possession of Dangerous weapon. Subject served two years in Sing Sing, and was wanted for violation of parole, Parole Officer, Albert Schwartz, # 148.

(2)

6. During the performance of a duty requiring police action above and beyond that expected of a trainee of Rosen's years and police experience, Trainee Rosen exhibited a degree of intelligence, skillful application, and a keen grasp of the unusual police situation that marks him as a splendid example of potential recruit material. Request that the proper department recognition be conferred.

Stanley A. Cafaro
Lieutenant

REPORT UNDER
R&P 26/7.0

U. F. 49

POLICE DEPARTMENT

NEW YORK, N.Y. 10013

September 8, 1970

From: Commanding Officer, 106th Precinct

To: The Police Commissioner

Subject: REQUEST FOR DEPARTMENTAL RECOGNITION:
           POLICE TRAINEE GARY ROSEN I.D. #60834, 106TH PRECINCT

1.   Police Trainee Gary Rosen I.D. #60834, assigned to the
106th Precinct, on June 4, 1970, by clever and alert thinking, supplied
information that led to an arrest of one male for Robber, 1st Degree
and possession of a Dangerous Weapon.

2.   One June 4, 1970 while Trainee Rosen was performing tour
of duty from 0001-0800 hours as telephone switchboard operator, he
received a call on an outside wire from a unknown male who asked if the
police knew about a holdup of a Bar and Grill on Metropolitan Avenue.
During the conversation Trainee Rosen sensed that the caller, from the
way he spoke, was implicated in the crime. Keeping him in conversation
Trainee Rosen managed to get the caller's name and location. The
Trainee then asked the caller to call back in about thirty minutes and
he would have the information he wanted concerning the holdup.
In the thirty minute interim, Trainee Rosen contacted the Criminal
Identification Bureau, where a check of the caller's name matched an
individual with a previous criminal record. Trainee Rosen then contacted the 106 Squad, briefed them on what took place. Two detectives
from the 106 Squad along with two detectives from the 104th Squad, as
location was within the 104th Precinct, went to the location and on
arrival, the suspect was in conversation with Trainee Rosen. After
investigation, the suspect, one Berard Kissane, Male, White, 43 of
270 First Avenue, Mineola, was arrested and charged with Robber 1st
degree and Possession of a Dangerous Weapon (.22 calibre Pistol).
The robbery took placd at 79-56 Metropolitan Avenue, Queens, a
Bar and Grill owned by Thomas Schutz of 66-75 73rd Place, Queens,
who was also the complaining witness. Arrest #569, 104th precinct.
Arresting Officer, Detective Roman Shield #2129, 104th Squad.

3.   Trainee Rosen through his exceptional and creditable acts
has reflected credit to this department, therefore recommend that
he be considered for departmental recognition in the proper degree
for his contribution to a valuable police service.

                          William McGarry
epk   Captain, 106th Precinct

U. F. 49

POLICE DEPARTMENT
CITY OF NEW YORK
NEW YORK, N. Y. 10013

May 4, 1971

Mr. Gary Rosen
26 Coleridge Street
Manhattan Beach,
Brooklyn, N.Y.

Dear Mr. Rosen:

      The Honor Committee of the Police Department
has awarded you a Police Department Civilian Commendation
Bar, together with a Certificate of Commendation, for
your heroic and unselfish act on June 4, 1970, when you
assisted members of the 106th Detective Squad in arresting
a felon.

      You are requested to appear at Police Head-
quarters, 240 Centre Street, New York City, Monday, June
7, 1971, at 11:00 A.M., at which time Police Commissioner
Patrick V. Murphy will present you with the Commendation
Bar and Certificate. Members of your family are also
invited to attend.

      Commissioner Murphy has asked me to express
his extreme gratitude for an outstanding example of
public service.

Sincerely,

Wilfred N. Horne
DEPUTY COMMISSIONER
PRESS RELATIONS

ads

P.S. - Kindly confirm your presence on June 7, by
     calling Patrolman Schoberl at Ca 6-3205 at
     your earliest convenience.

From:
POLICE DEPARTMENT, CITY OF NEW YORK   PATRICK V. MURPHY
Public Information Division   Commissioner
240 Centre Street
New York, N.Y. 10013
577-7432

- - - - - - - - - - - - - PRESS RELEASE - - - - - - - - - - - - - -

For Release: IMMEDIATELY   <u>MONDAY, JUNE 7, 1971</u>
                                  <u>NO. 51</u>

     Police Commissioner Patrick V. Murphy today presented
Civilian Commendation Bars and Certificates to fifteen civilians
who performed acts of bravery by coming to the aid of police in the
capture of dangerous criminals and in the rescue of people in need
of assistance. Loaded guns were involved in eight of the eleven
cases.

     Two of those honored are residents of Queens, two are from
Manhattan, six are from the Bronx, four from Brooklyn and one is a
resident of Yonkers.

     Occupations represented include a fireman, a police trainee,
a police administrative assistant, an employee of El Tiempo, a
postal employee, a bus driver, an owner of a real estate agency, a
fur buyer, two maintenance men, a truck driver, an accountant and a
gas station attendant.

     Those honored at the ceremony were:

MR. GARY ROSEN - On June 4, 1970, police trainee Rosen, on duty at
the 106th Precinct switchboard received a call from an unkown
man who asked if the police knew anything about a robbery of a bar
and grill. Sensing that the caller was implicated in the crime, he
kept him in conversation, obtained the callers name and address and
told him he would call him back in half an hour to give him the information. Trainee Rosen then called the 106th Squad and the Identification Section. Two detectives went to the callers residence and
found him again in conversation with trainee Rosen. Investigation
resulted in his arrest for this robbery and possession of a .22
calibre pistol..

POLICE DEPARTMENT

CITY OF NEW YORK

OFFICE OF THE POLICE COMMISSIONER

New York, July 26, 1971.

SPECIAL ORDERS NO. 129.

1—The following Police Trainees having satisfactorily completed service as such trainees in accordance with Section 434a-8.0 of the Administrative Code, having reached the age of twenty-one years and having passed a medical examination were appointed to the position of Patrolman on Probation in the Police Department of the City of New York, at $9,499. per annum, and were assigned to the Police Academy, Recruits' Training School.

Effective July 15, 1971:

		Date of Birth	Shield No.
Pilar Ferrer	865620	7- 7-50	13461
Thomas M. Quigley	865621	7- 4-50	8581
Gary M. Rosen	865622	7- 5-50	13112
John C. Snidersich	865623	6-25-50	26445

2—The following named Probationary Patrolmen having completed their course of training in the Police Academy, Recruits' Training School, are assigned to Precincts specified:

To take effect 0800, July 28, 1971:

		To Pct.
Anthony R. Centrone	865601	25
Leonard W. D'Alessandro		
	865603	9
Steven J. Fajardo	865605	7
Richard A. Fusaro	865607	75
Timothy P. Gallagher	865608	79
Henry F. Stumpf III	865617	73

3—Following **Transfers** and **Assignments** are ordered:

Captain

To take effect 0800, July 28, 1971:

Daniel J. McGowan 823960, from Internal Affairs Division to Public Morals Administrative Division.

Lieutenants

To take effect 0800, July 27, 1971:

George P. Smith 822236, from 60th Precinct to 11th Division, assigned to Precinct duty.

To take effect 0800, July 28, 1971:

Daniel T. Kelly 830912, from 120th Precinct to 4th Division, assignment changed from Desk duty to Supervisor of Plainclothes Patrolmen.

Chapter Three

My first assignment as a uniformed patrolman in July of 1971 was with the 79th Precinct in Brooklyn's Bedford Stuyvesant, often referred to as "a real shithouse".

Due to the shortage of policemen at the time, coupled by the men sent off to the Vietnam War, some of us received "occupational deferments" disallowing the military to take us off police duty. This was only applied to officers who lived within New York City's five boroughs. We were, in fact, fighting our own war on the streets of the city, as radical groups (and others) targeted the men in blue. Some on the force were specifically assigned to protect the precinct houses and their parking lots from both random and organized violence and vandalism.

When I was first assigned to the 79, I learned a new term. I had been working the midnight shift, including weekends, and I tried to get a Saturday night off. I must've tried 3 or 4 times, dutifully filling out the UF28 request form, as instructed. Having been rejected each time for my request for a day off, I was determined to get an explanation. One night, after completing my shift at 8am, I waited at the station house for the arrival of the Roll Call patrolman, who was responsible for the scheduling of all the shifts. He was supposed to be there at 8 o'clock to do the 8-4 shift. Eight o'clock came and went, then 8:30, 8:45. Finally, at 9 o'clock, the guy enters the station house and I approached him, introducing myself. I explained that I'd submitted multiple requests for a Saturday night off, including the UF28 forms. "You're missing a form," he said. "What form?," I asked. "A US5. Attach a US5 to the UF28 next time." It took me a moment to understand what he was telling me. Apparently, the custom was to paper clip a 5 dollar bill to the UF28 form. I did so thereafter, and had no further trouble with my time off requests.

During my initial months at the 79 I accumulated a record of making many arrests. This caught the attention of the new, young Sergeant Harrison, in charge of the 4th Platoon, operating on a shift from 6 pm – 2 am Sergeant Harrison invited me to join the 4th Platoon, hoping that I might bring some "new blood" to the unit and increase the rate of arrests.

"I'm not sure," I told the Sergeant.

Harrison then asked, "What do you want ?"

"I want a seat," I answered simply, meaning a patrol car assignment, instead of foot beat.

As there was only one patrol car assigned to the 6 – 2 shift, I was asking a good bit for someone new to the force, and the only rookie on the team. Sgt. Harrison looked me over and asked: "Will you make collars for me?" I, of course, assured him that I would.

No one matched my eagerness to perform. Most patrolmen on this shift either had other jobs, as well, or were attending school during the day. As a result, few arrests had been made by this group, who were rumored to "kill time" in "safe areas." Periodically someone came in late, or simply didn't show up for his shift, and another cop (usually his partner) would cover for him, putting a "scratch" in the book, indicating that the absent patrolman had been on duty.

In high crime precincts, like the 79th, we often worked in "Salt & Pepper" teams – a white cop paired with a black cop. During one such pairing, my partner and I got a radio call from CB (Communications Bureau) to respond to a female who'd been stabbed in the neck. A large crowd had amassed, and upon arrival we sought to interview the victim, in the center of this mass.

My partner was Al Russell, a black officer. He and I were doing the 4-12 shift when we got the call. We managed to get to the girl who was stabbed, who told us she was stabbed by another woman. But, as we began to interview her, Al was attacked and knocked to the ground. Seeing this, I thought to myself, "Why are they assaulting a black cop?" A moment later a garbage can was thrust over my head, as the attackers included me as the focus of their fury. We managed to call in a 10-13 (officers seeking assistance) and were accorded a rapid response.

Suddenly, some 30 police officers wielding nightsticks waded into the crowd, seeking to rescue their brothers in blue. Our lives were indeed in peril. The arriving cops dispersed the crowd, and Al and I, a bit surprised by the quick response of support, were indeed grateful and relieved.
We both were transported to the hospital by radio car, to get checked out. Having sustained a slight concussion, I was put on sick report,.

I was determined to make arrests, and when I got my "seat" I made plenty of arrests. My time as a uniformed officer with the 79 was both foot patrol and radio car. Very early in 1972, I was transferred to the Organized Crime Control Bureau, Narcotics Division, Undercover Unit.

Last day in 79th precinct

Part Two
Undercover

Assigned to Organized Crime Control Bureau
Narcotics Division / Undercover Unit / 1st Precinct at Old Slip

Chapter Four

I began with the Organized Crime Control Bureau, Narcotics Division, Undercover Unit, stationed at the 1st Precinct, Old Slip, Manhattan. In the spring of 1972 I was assigned to Brooklyn South Narcotics. For this assignment I had received narcotics training and training for the use of several types of undercover guns.

Regarding this assignment, my father again sought to discourage me when I told him I was going into Narcotics, now begging me not to take the Undercover Narcotics (UC) position. My father, being from "the old school", felt that "some officers go there to make money." He told me, "You go into Narcotics, and they'll take you out in handcuffs." Bribery, confiscation and other shady practices were especially prevalent in the S.I.U. (Special Investigation Unit). They were located on the 4th floor at Old Slip: Undercover was stationed on the 3rd floor of the same building.

Other cops within the Narcotics Division who were straight and did a good job got "jammed up" for failing to inform on fellow officers involved in corruption. This reluctance to inform on fellow officers was referred to as the "Blue Wall". Cops didn't "give up" other cops, for fear of being considered a "rat".

Of the 30,000 cops on the job, Undercover consisted of one-per-one thousand – 30 men. The unit was broken down into ethnic divisions, to help infiltrate different ethnic gangs involved in illegalities: Black, Hispanic, Italian, Irish, and one Jew. He was

Howie Farkas, who left undercover to become an Investigator in Manhattan South Narcotics.

The Knapp Commission, still in progress, was concluding its work and Narcotics was perhaps the most dangerous of all police callings.

When most children are growing up they often long to present as more mature than their actual age. Hanging out with kids somewhat older, they pose as "big guys", seeking to enhance their reputations. It was a common practice for many youths to fabricate (or borrow from a senior friend) I.D. allowing them to purchase beer or wine, or to drink at bars before they were of legal age.

There are times, though, when appearing younger gives one an advantage. Thus it was with my assignment as an undercover cop for Brooklyn South Narcotics.

I'll explain how these undercover operations worked.

First, a complaint involving narcotics would be reported to the police department, which would be forwarded to the Organized Crime Control Bureau (O.C.C.B). The OCCB was comprised of two divisions: the Narcotics Division; and the Public Morals Division. Obviously, such a complaint would be sent to Narcotics, who would look over the complaint. They would identify the precinct that the complaint emanated from, and what District it fell under – in Brooklyn South, the 10th, 11th and 12th Districts. Each district was headed by a Lieutenant, who had several Sergeants (usually three) who ran Field Teams, consisting of 4-6 members. A team would investigate the complaint, if deemed legitimate, and approach an undercover cop to start a buy operation.

As an undercover narcotics cop, I infiltrated the world of drug dealers and was responsible for making drug buys alone. There were six undercover officers assigned to Brooklyn South, representing several ethnic groups. Sometimes I was introduced to dealers by a Confidential Informant (CI). CI's were people who had already been busted for drugs and were given the option of working with the police, by turning informant. This meant that they could be on probation, theoretically for their lifetimes, instead of facing prison time of up to 25 years. If an Undercover "turned a CI", the informant would be assigned to work with a different UC for reasons of safety. As the original UC was the sole member of the police force who the dealer-turned CI had directly sold to, he was the only one able to testify to the crime firsthand. So, in case I later became identified and "outed" as a cop by a CI, my life would be at risk. If I were to disappear, there'd be no witness to testify against the seller.

So, while I was working narcotics undercover, I also always had a Field Operations backup team assigned to help protect me. The backup team became more directly involved in each case at the time arrests were made. As in sports, teamwork was essential.

A formal Complaint Report, dated March 24, 1972 noted a call received by the police from an anonymous male "that one Alex Jackson M,N,19, alias 'Rabbit' is selling narcotics at 175 Lott St., first floor right." So began this undercover investigation in that neighborhood.

On April 14, 1972 I successfully completed an A "buy", or first buy from a dealer. This was an exchange I made (with an introduction by a female confidential informant) of cash for a bundle (10 bags) of heroin. When I returned – this time alone – to attempt a B, or second buy from the male dealer, the guy I got the bundle from was no longer there. I then bought nine bags of heroin from a different male dealer in the hallway of 133 Lott Street, Brooklyn, also an "A" buy. Two other young males entered the hallway, and the guy I'd bought the 9 bags from told the newcomers that I was "looking to buy a bundle" (10 bags) more of dope. "Alright, we'll take care of you," said one. I agreed to the buy, but told them it couldn't be in the hallway.

The two accompanied me to my car, a Triumph Spitfire, where I sat at the wheel with one of the dealers across from me in the other front seat. The other dealer approached the open driver's window, punching me in the head, as the one next to me unfolded a knife and held it to my throat. The two then opened up on me, one punching me wherever he could land a blow and pulling at the pockets of my clothes, searching for drugs and money. As I resisted, the one with the knife shoved it into my midsection. Fortunately, the knife's lock wasn't on, and I was wearing a new jacket of stiff denim material, so the blade folded back into the handle as the two fled from my car. They'd gotten $105 and six of the nine bags of heroin. I got out of the car to pursue them, a bit unsteady from the daze of the assault. Bleeding and dizzy, I started after them with my handgun drawn.

This was a predominantly black neighborhood, and soon telephone calls were coming in to the station that there was "a white man with a gun, running through the streets." It wasn't long before an unmarked car from the 67th Precinct's Anti-Crime Unit pulled up and two plainclothesmen jumped out with their guns drawn, ordering me to "Drop the weapon !" As I had a new Silver .25 Automatic (which I didn't want to damage), I responded: "I'm going to slowly put the gun on the ground." In short order I was able to convey to these two that I was on the job, undercover, while trying not to advertise to the neighborhood that I was a cop. The area was searched for the mutts who'd attacked me, to no avail.

Though subsequent investigation identified the person involved in the initial buy as Donald "Duck" Straton (2514 Beverly Road, Brooklyn - apprehended), the two others weren't identified definitively. Their descriptions: #1-M-N-17, 6'3", 160lbs., believed to be Eddie Battles l/k/a 133-12223rd St., Queens (no longer residing there); #2-M-N-17, 5'9", 135 lbs., wearing long black coat, blue dungarees, sneakers, no further information.

A Complaint Report #2439 was presented to the 67th Precinct, and "in view of the above circumstances," I requested that "$85.00 in U.S. currency be credited to the Narcotics Division, as this amount was 'Buy Money' and the remaining $20.00 was personal money."

So, not an entirely successful day at work. I'd been smacked around a bit, and was out 20 bucks, to boot. Yet, I'd learned from this encounter, and would be better prepared for future assignments.

As there was no narcotics unit stationed on Staten Island, Brooklyn South covered the entire Island, and I and the other undercover cop working with me, Nicholas Molfetta, were responsible for all the undercover narcotics buys. I was quite a sight. To blend in with the hippie drug scene I'd grown long hair and a full beard. My outfits were consistent with the elements I immersed myself in: jeans, with a big belt buckle, multi-layered combinations of shirts, vests and jackets, accentuated by "cool" scarves. I often wore a hat, and had a suede shoulder bag with fringe, completing my frayed image. I was just another young "head", looking to score.

In the summer of 1972, prominently noted in articles published in the New York Post and Staten Island Advance, we scored a major bust on Staten Island in a series of raids. By Tuesday, July 18th, 21 arrests of young men and women were made on the Island during six days of raids, netting $500,000 worth of heroin, LSD, cocaine and other drugs. The raids were conducted by agents from District Attorney John M. Braisted Jr.'s office and 38 policemen from our Brooklyn South Narcotics borough command. All of the "buys" which set up these raids were purchased by me and Nick, separately, in an undercover capacity. In addition to my infiltration, we used wiretapping and observation trucks. No listening devices were planted, because we feared that they might be discovered, blowing the operation.

These arrests became landmark trials for the early 1970's, as presiding Judge Leon Becker demanded exceedingly high bail – for those days – and admonished defendants' attorneys who sought leniency for their young clients. In response to one defense lawyer asking the judge not to "peremptorily punish" his client with such stringent bail, Judge Becker spoke of his first-hand awareness of the devastation drugs were responsible for within communities. "Counselor, come to the Lower East Side where I live and see the human misery there sometime," said the judge. "People often claim you can buy drugs anywhere, but nobody does anything about it. Well, I'm going to do something about it."

At that time organized crime was developing a foothold in Staten Island, and authorities were determined to intercede in the blossoming distribution of drugs there. Though "soft drugs" (considered relatively harmless) like marijuana had been prevalent in upper-class neighborhoods, the increase of LSD and "hard drugs" like speed and heroin being sold on and out of Staten Island became a major concern.

It was while working in Staten Island that I first heard the term "White Lady". When I was attempting to purchase narcotics from a dealer, asking if he had heroin or cocaine, he asked me, "Do you mean White Lady?" This was a street term for cocaine that had originated back in the 1930s. My undercover image served me – and the Department – well, so my role as a drug-seeker continued.

COMPLAINT REPORT (PD 313-152 (Rev. 10-71) (FORMERLY U. F. 61)	*FOR OFFICE USE ONLY (Do Not Fold This Report)		Additional Copies Required For:						Complaint File No.

Complainant's Surname	First Name	Business Phone	6. Date and Time Reported		14 *	15 *	19. Pct.	22. Compl. No.
People			3/24/72	0815			67	1843

Complainant's Address — Residence Phone — Apt. No. — 11. Day, Date and Time of Occurrence: **various times during day** — 16 * — 17 * — 27. Post **B** — 30. C.C.D. No. **187440**

Offense (if any): **Investigate- Narcotics** — 36 * — 39 * — 40 * — 41 * — 42. Pct of Arrest — 45. Arrest Nos.

Place of Occurrence: ☒ Inside ☐ Outside
175 Lott St. 1st floor right

	50. Type of Property ☐ Lost ☐ Stolen	51. Value of Property	57. Value of Property Recovered
Type of Premises, Business, etc. **dwelling - Apt. House**	1. Autos Stolen or Recovered		
Alarm No. — Pct. — Date and Time Transmitted	2. ☐ Autos Recovered by Other Auth. 3. ☐ For Other Auth.		
	4. Currency		
	5. Jewelry		
Referred to **O.C.C.B.** — 64.*	6. Furs		
	7. Clothing		
Closed by Uniform Force ☐ Yes ☒ No — Desk Officer's Rank/Signature **Sgt.**	8. Firearms		
	9. Miscellaneous		

Witness's Surname	First Name	Address and Apt. No.	Residence Phone	Business Phone
1.				
2.				

PERPETRATOR'S DESCRIPTION — Victim will view photos ☐ Yes ☐ No

Sex	Color	Age	Hgt.	Wgt.	Hair	Eyes	Complexion	Other(Scars, Tattoo, Clothes, etc.)
1.								
2.								
3.								

PERSONS ARRESTED:	Surname	First Name	Address and Apt. No.	City
1.				
2.				

DETAILS AS REPORTED BY COMPLAINANT AND/OR INITIAL INVESTIGATING OFFICER
Received by telephone from anonymous male caller that one **Alex Jackson** M,N,19, alias "Rabbit" is selling narcotics at place of occurrence. Complt further states that there is unusually large amount of pedestrian traffic entering and leaving said apartment.
OCCB- Ptl. Kennedy notified- #2-4908

USE REVERSE SIDE IF MORE SPACE IS NEEDED (Carbon must be inverted)

VEHICLE USED	Make	Year	Color	License No.	State	Body Style	Other Characteristics
WEAPONS USED	☐ Revolver ☐ Automatic ☐ Rifle	Caliber	Knife (Describe)				Other (Specify)
EVIDENCE	☐ None ☐ Personal Belongings ☐ Narcotics ☐ Tools ☐ Other	Specify					

DESCRIPTION OF LOST OR STOLEN PROPERTY - See Appendix G of R. & P. | Property Clerk Voucher No.

Article (Name Only)	Quantity	Value	Description (Include Serial Numbers Where Possible)

Initial Investigating Officer's Name (Typed) Rank — Name — Shield No. — Command	Investigating Officer's Signature	Precinct Commander's Signature Rank — Name — Command

DISTRICT SPECIALIZED SQUAD COPY

U. F. 49
P.D. 188-151

POLICE DEPARTMENT

NEW YORK, N. Y. 10013

April 16, 1972

From: Patrolman Gary Rosen, Shield 13112, Undercover,
Narcotics Borough Brooklyn South.

To: Bureau of Audits and Accounts, Director.

Subject: ASSAULT AND ROBBERY OF UNDERCOVER PATROLMAN ASSIGNED
TO NARCOTICS DIVISION.

1. On April 14, 1972, the undersigned performed tour of
duty 1000 to 1800hours, and assigned to Buy Operation #203. At
about 1655hours, date indicated, I was assaulted and robbed of
$105.00 in U.S. currency and six bags of alleged heroin, which
was being held as evidence. The circumstances of the assault
and robbery are as follows:

At about 1645hours, April 14, 1972, I had just completed the purchase of nine bags of alleged heroin from an
unknown male in the hallway of 133 Lott Street, Brooklyn, when
two other unknown males entered the hallway and the first male
told them that I was looking for a "bundle", more heroin. The
two males offered to sell more heroin to me and I agreed to
buy but not in the hallway. The two males accompanied me to my
auto and the three of us entered the car and sat in the front
seat. At this point, the male seated in the middle produced a
knife and held it to my throat and ordered me to drive away.

I drove to Veronica Place and Albemarle Road, Brooklyn,
and parked at the curb. The two perpetrators began punching me
and searching my pockets and clothing. As I resisted, the male
jabbed the knife into my stomach area, but the blade folded back
into the handle. During this struggle, this male took $105.00
in U.S. Currency and six of the nine bags of alleged heroin, the
money from my pants pocket and the alleged heroin from the right
pocket of my jacket.

The two males alighted from my car and proceeded to
flee the scene on foot. I attempted to pursue but was dazed by
the assault. Due to the crowded sidewalks at the scene, I
decided not to use my revolver.

2. The following named members of the force were assigned
as the back-up team in this operation:

Sergeant Frank Tilelli, shield 734, Supervisor, 10th
Narcotics District

- 2 -

Patrolmen James O'Neil, shield 26406; William Mulligan, shield 719; and Louis Mandasso, shield 12206, all assigned to the 10th Narcotics District

3. They were keeping the perpetrators and myself in sight during and after the initial buy and presumed that a second buy was taking place and were unable to observe the assault and robbery being purpetrated.

They followed in the direction I had taken and found me at Bedford Avenue and Albemarle Road in a dazed condition. The area was searched to no avail.

4. Subsequent investigation disclosed the identity of the person involved in the initial buy to be Donald Steven (Duck) Straton, 2314 Beverly Road, Brooklyn, apprehended.

5. The two males involved in the assault and robbery are described as:

#1-M-N-17, 6'1", 160lbs., believed to be Eddie Battles l/k/a 133-12 223rd Street, Queens (no longer resides thereat)
#2-M-N-17, 5'9", 135lbs., wearing long black coat, blue dungarees, sneakers, no further

6. Complaint Report #2439, 67th Precinct, prepared, Detective Robert J. DeMarzo, shield 1135, 13th D.D. Robbery, assigned. Alarm #12163 transmitted.

7. In view of the above circumstances, request that $65.00 in U.S. currency be credited to the Narcotics Division, as this amount was "Buy Money" and the remaining $20.00 was personal money.

Gary Rosen
Shield 13112
Undercover
Narcotics Borough Brooklyn

1st Endorsement

Sergeant Bernard Edwards, Shield 863, 12th Narcotics District, (Custodian of "Buy Money") to Commanding Officer, Narcotics Borough Brooklyn South, April 18, 1972. Sergeant Mikelli and other members of the force engaged in this operation conferred with and verified circumstances as stated above. Recommend $65.00 in U.S. currency be credited to the Narcotics Division.

Sgt Bernard E Edward
Bernard Edwards
Shield 863
12th Narcotics District

- 3 -

2nd Endorsement

Commanding Officer, Narcotics Borough Brooklyn South To Commanding
Officer, Narcotics Division, April 18, 1972. Contents noted.
Matter investigated and no evidence of negligence or violations
of the Rules and Procedures were found on the part of Patrolman
Rosen or Sergeant Tilelli or other members involved in this case.
Patrolman Rosen acted commendably in refraining from firing his
revolver in a crowded area. Recommend APPROVAL.

John F. Barry
Captain

jrn/

Weather
Tonight: Warm, humid.
Tomorrow: Hot, humid.

Vol. 87. No. 17,003   62 Pages   10 Cents

Staten Island Advance

Staten Island, N.Y., Wednesday, July 19, 1972

Final edition
★ ★ ★

Home-Delivered Daily & Sunday, 60c a week

21 nabbed in Island drug raids

$500,000 in narcotics seized

By WILLIAM REYCRAFT
and NEIL DRISCOLL

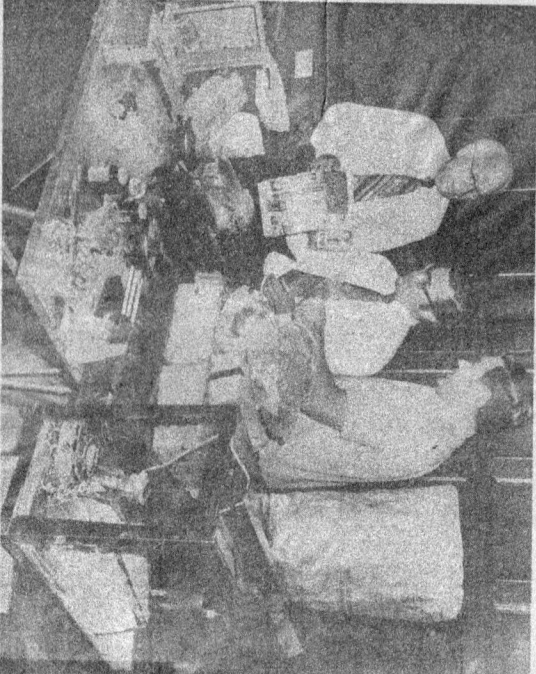

District Attorney John M. Braisted Jr., left, checks some of the material seized—including a boa constrictor—in a fish tank—during a series of narcotics raids on Staten Island. Helping with the inventory are Assistant District Attorney Thomas Lloyd, center, and Capt. Jeremiah O'Connor, commander of the Richmond-South Brooklyn narcotics squad.

S.I. Advance Photo by Tony Carannante

The
City
of
New York

POLICE DEPARTMENT

NEW YORK, N. Y. 10013

Narcotics Borough Brooklyn South
397 Coney Island Avenue
Brooklyn, New York 11226

May 23, 1973

Dr. Philip Groisser, Principal
Sheepshead Bay High School
3000 Avenue X
Brooklyn, New York

Dear Sir:

On April 11, 1973, a confidential investigation was initiated by our Department in connection with alleged narcotics trafficking by teachers of your school. Several anonymous telephone calls had been received at the Brooklyn District Attorney's Office alleging that five teachers were selling narcotics to students in your school. With the cooperation of several teachers in your school, we were able to send in an undercover police officer to investigate this matter.

The following members of your staff should receive the highest praise for their unquestionable dedication and integrity. They are truly a great asset to your school. They are:

Mr. William P. Brown; Mr. Lee Bergman; Mr. Daniel Walker, and Miss Susan Pokodner (although a substitute teacher, she showed an extreme amount of concern and great willingness to cooperate).

The results of this investigation proved the complaints to be unfounded. For this, we should all be thankful.

Thank you again for your cooperation and should you need our services in the future, please do not hesitate to contact this Office.

John Walsh
Lieutenant
Commanding Officer
10th Narcotics District

Chapter Five

After the Staten Island operation, I continued to work undercover, now in Brooklyn.

In a middle class neighborhood in Bay Ridge, a group of young adult men and women had reportedly been selling drugs for several months. On Friday, August 26th, 1972, raids took place headed by Captain Jeremiah O'Connor, the Commanding Officer of Brooklyn South Narcotics and Lieutenant Michael O'Shea of the 12th District Narcotics Squad.

Arrests were made in a two-part operation. Three people were arrested in an alleged "cutting factory", where more than an ounce of cocaine, barbiturates and narcotics paraphernalia (scales and packaging products) were confiscated, conducted by another cop working undercover. This apartment on Marine Avenue was where the sellers "stepped on" the cocaine they'd gotten, before distributing the "cut" product in street sales.

Minutes later, other portions of the team, utilizing a new tactic making street arrests, swept into Owl's Head Park at 68th Street and Colonial Road, arresting 12 of the street peddlers working for the dealers. I was the sole undercover on all these buys. Roughly $50,000 of cocaine, barbiturates, marijuana, LSD and hash oil were confiscated at the park. We dried up a major source of dope in Bay Ridge with these raids.

In undercover, I used this new tactic which made it easier for the field teams to make arrests. When I'd make buys from the dealers during the day, I'd initiate subtle physical contact with them. For the first time, I was equipped with a new method of identifying the dealers, which I employed. On my hands was a powder, not visible to the naked eye, but shining in fluorescent intensity under a black light. Later, in the evening, the arresting officers approached the suspects in the park. While some of them may no longer have been "carrying", having ditched their stash of drugs, when the police flashed their "secret weapon" – a portable black light – on the parts of clothing I'd marked with powder – these guys were caught.

Subsequent visits to Owl's Head Park by the field teams during the next week confirmed the success of our operation, as countless potential drug buyers searched the park, to no avail.

During the start of the school year in the fall of 1972 , I began undercover work at Sheepshead Bay High School. Still quite youthful looking and attired in convincing clothing, I fit in well at the school. Only the school Principal and one or two others were aware of my status as an undercover cop. One of the reasons I'd been assigned to work undercover at the high school was to determine if there was any truth to the rumor about teachers selling drugs to students.

In fact, I immersed myself so well into the student population that I earned the ire of one of the teachers who taught a class I was enrolled in. This teacher was an attractive young lady, perhaps in her early twenties, who had it in for the students who were using and selling drugs. She believed me to be one of those involved with drugs and she rode me hard.

"I'm going to call your mother, and you won't graduate," she threatened.

After I sought – and received – permission from the school Dean to let her in on my actual role at school, I waited for this teacher in my Triumph Spitfire after school one day. She walked out of school and saw me, but tried to avoid eye contact, so I called her over. "What do you want ?" she asked. "Get in the car," I told her, "I'm not going anywhere with you," she said. I asked if the Dean had spoken with her, vouching that she could trust me, and when she admitted to that discussion she reluctantly got into the passenger seat.

I drove us to a diner, telling her that I wanted to talk with her. When she said, "I'm not hungry," I suggested that she just order a cup of coffee.

Sitting across from her in one of the diner's booths, I asked her, "Do you know what I am ?"

"Yeah," she replied, "you're a drug dealer."

I corrected her with, "No, I'm an undercover cop."

The surprise on her face was genuine and she spat her coffee out. I assured her that I was a NYC policeman, working Undercover Narcotics and showed her my identification. Well, her attitude toward me altered radically. Not only was she no longer out to nail me, but she softened to the point of seeing me socially. We began a relationship which lasted for half a year.

I made 36 dope buys in the streets adjacent to the school, from the school dealers. The majority of sellers were students of Sheepshead Bay High School, while some were students from Erasmus Hall High School. One was a student from the John Jay College of Criminal Justice. Of the 16 arrests in this narcotics ring, on October 2, 1972, one stood out notably – a law clerk for the Manhattan D.A.'s office, Douglas Colbert. Mr. Colbert was a 24 year old honor graduate of Brooklyn Law School, who began work for the city on September 5, and was awaiting results of the bar examination he took in July. I made drug buys from Colbert's brother, which were sold to me at Douglas Colbert's house. Though Douglas was not present at the time, drug paraphernalia were seized at his house, including a very large bong.

Most of the drugs were bought on the 3000 block of Coyle Street, between Emmons Avenue and the Belt Parkway. The street consisted of two large apartment buildings. All of the dealers hung out on the street between these two buildings. I was using my Triumph Spitfire to make the buys. At his time, I was residing on the other side of the bay in Manhattan Beach.

Charges for the group included sales of heroin, cocaine, marijuana, hashish and LSD. Many of the students at the high school who were interviewed following the arrests downplayed the severity of drug use in the school. Some contested that marijuana, while illegal, was not a dangerous drug. In fact, most students estimated that 90% of those in high school had smoked pot at least once. Still, some of the students did favor punishment for "pushers".

There was one parent, the father of Alan Michaels, whose reaction to the arrest of his son was memorable. This man was one of the parents who'd very vocally been prompting the police to make more arrests, to "clean up this drug problem in our neighborhood." Before the arrests, Mr. Michaels called the precinct repeatedly to say that "drugs were running rampant at school." Following the arrests, he went to the precinct where the suspects were held for booking and raised holy hell.

"How dare they lock my son up. He hasn't done anything wrong," he shouted. "I've been the one pushing to get the dealers. They got the wrong people."

In fact, I had made A, B, C and D buys from this young man, meaning that he'd sold drugs to me on four documented occasions. The father's incessant harassment of the police served as inspiration to make the kid's major drug involvement well-evidenced. On the fourth (D) buy, the kid had carelessly packaged LSD pills, wrapping them in his own W-2 Tax Form, with his name and home address printed clearly on the sheet He handed this package to me, in exchange for cash. When this W-2 Form package of acid was presented as evidence, the unsuspecting Mr. Michaels was forced to reevaluate his naive trust in his son's behaviors.

On May 23, 1973 the Commanding Officer of the 10th Narcotics District, Lieutenant John Walsh, wrote to the Principal of Sheepshead Bay High School, Dr. Philip Groisser, detailing the results of an undercover operation that began on April 11, 1973. This investigation was initiated when the Brooklyn District Attorney's office received several anonymous calls, alleging that five teachers were selling narcotics to students at the school. I was sent in, as an undercover police officer, to investigate this matter. Lt. Walsh's letter offered the "highest praise" for the teachers under suspicion, based upon my findings. He concluded that "The results of this investigation proved the complaints unfounded. For this, we should be thankful."

These multiple high school drug busts earned me and a number of other patrolmen, detectives and a sergeant commendations. On February 19, 1973 the Police Department,

City of New York issued Personnel Order No. 69, DEPARTMENTAL RECOGNITION, which noted that we were "hereby awarded EXCELLENT POLICE DUTY, in accordance with the provisions of T.O.P. 129,1972," with my Date of Occurrence September 9, 1972. On February 22, 1973 a similar DEPARTMENTAL RECOGNITION, this time for Personnel Order No. 76 was issued to four patrolmen, including my undercover partner, Nicholas Molfetta, two other detectives and myself, with the Date of Occurrence of July 18, 1972, involving the buy operation on Staten Island.

By the time we'd received these recognitions, we were already working a spin-off operation.

THE NEW YORK TIMES, TUESDAY, OCTOBER 3, 1972

A CITY LAW CLERK SEIZED AS PUSHER

Accused With 15 Youths of Drug Sales to Brooklyn High School Students

By MORRIS KAPLAN

A law clerk for the city's Corporation Counsel was linked yesterday by District Attorney Eugene Gold of Brooklyn to a narcotics ring that specialized in selling drugs to students at Sheepshead Bay High School.

The clerk was identified as Douglas Colbert, a 24-year-old honor graduate of Brooklyn Law School who began working for the city Sept. 5 and is awaiting results of a bar examination he took in July.

Accused of selling $120 worth of marijuana and possessing one ounce of it, Mr. Colbert was arrested along with 15 Brooklyn youths on charges of drug sales in the high-school area. Three of these sold heroin and four others cocaine, while the others peddled hashish, marijuana or LSD, Mr. Gold charged. All came from middle-class families, he said.

Three suspects were identified as Sheepshead Bay High School students, two as students at Erasmus Hall High School in Flatbush and another as a student at the John Jay College of Criminal Justice.

Inquiry Pending

Mr. Colbert qualified for his $11,400-a-year post by passing a Civil Service examination. He placed 36th on a list of 172 applicants, a spokesman for the Corporation Counsel disclosed. The spokesman said Mr. Colbert would not be suspended, pending a departmental investigation.

The police said that Mr. Colbert, of 1060 Ocean Avenue, in the Parkville section of Brooklyn, could receive a maximum prison sentence of 15 years if convicted.

His 16-year-old brother, Monte, a student at Sheepshead Bay High School who lives with his parents at 5810 Farragut Road, was charged with selling cocaine, hashish and marijuana. If convicted he also could get 15 years.

Mr. Gold said the ringleader was Jay Greber, 21, of 580

The New York Times/Barton Silverman

Some of the suspects in the Sheepshead Bay High School drug case being taken from a police truck to court yesterday in downtown Brooklyn.

15 years.

Mr. Gold said the ringleader was Jay Greber, 21, of 580 East 17th Street, Flatbush, charged with selling marijuana on two occasions. His apartment was used as a "factory" to process the drug, the prosecutor said.

More Arrests Expected

The arrests were made early yesterday, except for that of Melville Braham, who was taken into custody Friday on the school's premises at 3000 Avenue X.

Mr. Braham, who lives at 1384 Sterling Place, in the Brownsville section, was released in $1,000 bail in Brooklyn Criminal Court on charges of having sold heroin on two occasions.

Mr. Gold said an investigation into narcotics sales at Sheepshead Bay High School began in June, prompted by "a citizen's complaint." He predicted "possibly four additional arrests."

Some sales, he said, were made inside the school but most transactions took place "either

All have been readmitted as students after having completed treatment in rehabilitation centers. The school has an active drug-abuse program, the principal said, in which addicts have been referred to methadone agencies or to such centers as Phoenix House and Samaritan House.

Seized on a charge of possessing a loaded .22-caliber gun was Martin Kahn, 24, of 510 Ocean Parkway. Conviction carries a possible maximum term of four years.

The others and the charges against them were the following:

Robert Levey, 22 of 100 Avenue P, Bensonhurst, a freelance musician, two sales of cocaine.

Howard Lipson, 18, same address; two sales of cocaine.

Jacob Levy, 17 of 1060 Ocean Avenue, a student at Erasmus Hall High School; selling heroin and hashish.

Gary Solomon, 21 of 385 Argyle Road, Flatbush, a laborer, selling heroin.

Alan Michaels, 16, of 2800

Coyle Street, a Sheepshead Bay High-School student; selling cocaine, LSD and marijuana.

Lee Katz, 23, of 510 Ocean Parkway; selling marijuana.

Howard Parlman, 20, of 659 East Fifth Street, a truck driver who graduated from the New York School of Printing; selling marijuana.

Lee Wolf, 18, of 2815 Coyle Street, a student at the John Jay College of Criminal Justice; selling marijuana.

David Nagashina, 16, of 2800 Coyle Street, a Sheepshead Bay High School student; selling hashish and possession of marijuana.

Mark Lifschitz, 23, of 490 Ocean Parkway, who attended Brooklyn College for 2½ years; selling marijuana.

Philip Lifschitz, his brother, 17, a student at Erasmus Hall High School; selling marijuana.

POLICE DEPARTMENT
CITY OF NEW YORK

Personnel Order No. 69   February 19, 1973

DEPARTMENTAL RECOGNITION

Departmental Recognition is awarded to the following members of the service for meritorious conduct performed in the line of duty:

1. The following named members are hereby awarded EXCELLENT POLICE DUTY, in accordance with the provisions of T.O.P. 129,1972.

RANK	NAME	TAX REG #	COM'D	DATE OF OCCURR
Sgt	Edward Mamet	842358	10 DD ROB	8/1/72
Det	Daniel J. Kelleher	844949	"	"
Det	August Maurina	837498	"	"
Det	Robert Marshall	848046	"	"
Sgt	John J. Meehan	845681	10 ND	9/29/72
Ptl	Sheldon Wasserman	849697	"	"
Ptl	Mario M. Martino	852913	"	"
Ptl	Charles Goffredo	860470	"	"
Ptl	Gary Rosen	865622	"	"

POLICE DEPARTMENT
CITY OF NEW YORK

Personnel Order No. 76   February 22, 1973

DEPARTMENTAL RECOGNITION

Departmental Recognition is awarded to the following members of the service for meritorious conduct performed in the line of duty:

1. The following named members are hereby awarded MERITORIOUS POLICE DUTY, in accordance with the provisions of T.O.P. 129,1972.

Det	Brendan Feeley	848583	10 ND	7/18/72
Det	Joseph Monahan	835594	"	"
Ptl	Donald Anderson	852181	"	"
Ptl	Nicholas Molfetta	862481	"	"
Ptl	Stephen Spinelli	855483	1 ND	"
Ptl	Gary Rosen	865622	NBBS	"

Chapter Six

We "graduated from high school to college," in our pursuit of youthful drug offenders, as our investigations spread to Brooklyn College in 1973. A four-month investigation of narcotics sales to students culminated on February 25, 1973, when 21 persons were arrested on drug charges. Along with Brooklyn College, illegal sales had been made to students at Kingsborough Community College, Midwood High School and Ditmas Junior High School.

In all, four independent rings, operating separately, were responsible for narcotics sales. The raids took place from 6 pm on the 25th through 3 am on the 26th. I had completed buys from these groups of sellers before the raids were carried out.

The major pusher caught was a 26 year old named Robert Hollis, a Baruch College law student who lived with Modesto Calderon. Calderon, a Transit Authority (TA) Police Officer on duty for 8 years, was suspended immediately after his arrest. At the home where he and his roommate (Hollis) were busted, police seized 25 pounds of marijuana, 8 ounces of cocaine, a .22 caliber revolver and a bankbook showing deposits of $10,000, along with $2000 in cash.

In this operation, I had been purchasing major weight buys from light-skinned black Hollis (raised by a Jewish family) in his brownstone apartment. Unknown to me, TA Police Officer Calderon, hidden behind a pocket door, had allegedly had a shotgun trained on me during the transactions. My backup men related this to me. If he'd sensed something going wrong with Hollis and me, like me ripping him off, his job was to open up with the shotgun.

Hollis subsequently attempted to gain an exception with these charges, as a felony conviction would negate his seeking the ability to obtain a law license. I was contacted years later and asked for my opinion: I strongly opposed allowing this exception.

A Psychology student at Brooklyn College, Michael DeCastro (28) was arrested on a charge of selling LSD and hashish. Though College officials deny that DeCastro was a drug counselor, I had attended several drug counseling groups at the school that were conducted by DeCastro. He was noted for suggesting to students that the "cure" for getting off their heroin addictions was to use LSD. Prematurely bald, DeCastro was referred to as "Maharishi Mike".

An 11 year old student introduced us to two 14 year old pushers who'd sold us drugs, and were arrested with the others. Brooklyn District Attorney (D.A.) Eugene Gold's office referred these youths to Family Court. It was estimated that these distributors netted $500,000 a year, just from the sales to students at the aforementioned schools.

D.A. Gold was not unlike most of those who are politically appointed, and sought to take credit whenever doing so might enhance his career. I attended a Shomrim meeting at which Gold was the guest speaker. During his speech he began to tell of how he and his detectives had taken down the school drug operations, without even crediting the police department.

I stood up to interrupt, asking Gold: "Do you know who I am ?" He said "No." I announced my name, and told him – and all others present – "On those busts, I was by myself. Your office was involved in the prosecution, but had nothing to do with the buys." Sometimes, you just can't stay silent.

In fact, D.A. Gold had sought to involve his office earlier, as a joint operation. He was initially told no by Captain O'Conner. But Gold went to the higher-ups in the Department, who then put pressure and forced the Captain to allow him to participate.

An aside to the college drug bust operation was an unexpected family encounter. As one of the arrests was a result of the final buys, I was present during the time they arrested the dealers and was taken into custody with the pushers who had been selling dope.

Those of us under arrest were brought upstairs to the 70th Detective Squad. The responsibility for gathering fingerprints fell on the detective squads. As I stood in the "cage" with the others, my father, Detective Russell Rosen, who was assigned to the 70th Detective Squad and was working that night, came in and reached through the bars of the cage, grabbing me by my beard, saying, "Will you look at this mutt?!?"

I shouted, "Fuck you, cop!"

My dad then let go. Of the two other detectives in the room, Tommy Cerbone knew me, but the other – an Irishman, known for drinking a bit, who shall remain unnamed here – opened the cage, dragged me out and began beating on me with a blackjack.

Cerbone did his best to stop the other detective from pummeling me, telling him, "That's Russ's son, you can't do that."

"I don't give a fuck who he is. He can't talk to a cop like that," and proceeded to finish me off with a couple more licks.

The only good result for me was that the criminals were well convinced that I wasn't a cop, when my bruised self was thrown back into the cage.

It was not long after this encounter that my father, Detective Russell Rosen retired in 1973. A friend of Dad's, Heshy Dembin had recently retired from the 9th Precinct in Manhattan and was working as Head of Security for Bonwit Teller. He'd told my father that there was an opening as the Head of Security for Gucci. Dad was offered, and took the position. At this time Aldo Gucci was in charge of the enormously successful fashion brand, founded by his father, Guccio Gucci in 1921.

My father found the job less rewarding than he'd anticipated, so he decided to return to police work. When retiring, my father was given the one year grace period which was afforded those who retired in good standing. If the retiree wished, he could rejoin the force within a year's time. That's exactly what my dad did, coming back to work at the 61st Detective Squad, from which he retired permanently from the NYC Police Dept. in 1975.

Captain Jeremiah O'Connor, whose crew was known as O'Connor's Raiders, became legendary in the department. In many raids, he was the first at the door of a bust – shotgun in hand. When he'd see me, he'd often ask: "What did you do for me today ?", and I'd tell him about my recent operations. He was as demanding of himself as he was of the cops under his command, and he was always supportive. He took no crap from anyone below or from those higher up in the ranks. At one time, the number of narcotics busts by O'Connor's crew far outdistanced those of other boroughs, including Brooklyn North, Manhattan South, Manhattan North, Bronx and Queens, all of whom had more men and bigger territories. He was even asked to "Slow down a bit. You're making the rest of us look bad." But of course he (and we) didn't. Eventually, they decided to cut funding to O'Connor's Raiders, drying up the "buy money" needed to purchase narcotics. Eventually, Captain O'Connor was taken out of his position and reassigned, where his successes were no longer an embarrassment to others with less initiative.

O'Connor was the best boss I ever worked for, and he and I became good friends. If I was working a night shift and needed a shower, I had Captain O'Connor's permission to use the shower adjacent to his office. Since I knew where he had a bottle of vodka stashed in a desk drawer, I'd sometimes help myself to a bit of his vodka, refill the bottle with water, and return it to his desk drawer. I'm not sure if anyone else was close enough to him – or ballsy enough – to get away with some of the things I did. I admired Jeremiah O'Connor, and I think of him, to this day. We remained close friends, even after I'd retired and moved to Florida.

Separate from the school operations, in June 1973, we arrested a Junior High School English teacher and a custodian working at the same school in Brownsville, Brooklyn for drug sales.

I had gotten an introduction to this teacher by posing as a Vietnam Veteran who was hoping to become a teacher myself. The teacher, Richard Kaplan (27), checked up on me before he let me get too close to him. We'd set up a phony telephone number, masquerading as part of the V.A. program. When Kaplan called, John Plansker (Captain and Commanding Officer of Brooklyn South Narcotics) picked up (in the role of a V.A. counselor) and vouched for me.

Kaplan had been a teacher for 4 years when he was charged with selling pills and LSD on March 26. Kaplan had introduced me to the school custodian, Spencer Huston (29), who sold me an ounce of pot out of Kaplan's apartment a few days later. On the wall of Kaplan's apartment was a poster, popular with the hippie culture of that time. It was a take-off of the red and white Coca Cola logo – this one promoting "Enjoy Cocaine" in the logo's lettering. Unfortunately, these drug busts never translated to connections "up the chain" to bigger distributors.

The conclusion of the school buy operation did include a dramatic incident which led us to a building within the confines of the 88th Precinct, Brooklyn North, a location that was part of the supply chain for heroin to the schools.

We had worked these buy operations for many months, and had arrived at the day when arrests were to be made. I was the sole undercover, working with field teams who not only protected me, but investigated the identities of the dealers. The procedure began with me making my final buys, with my backup team members arresting the perps immediately thereafter. Those who made the arrests were members of the 10th, 11th and 12th Narcotics Districts that made up Brooklyn South Narcotics.

Working with a new Confidential Informant (CI) for the first time, without a partner to accompany me on this big buy, the CI took me to a slum tenement building on Clausen Avenue. To enter, we had to go through a side door, down to the basement, then walk up five flights to where the dealers were. When we got there and the door opened I could see that this was more than a distribution site. People were scattered throughout the apartment, with some of them already nodding out. This was a "shooting gallery" where everyone was injecting the heroin they'd just purchased. This wasn't supposed to have been the scene, as CIs were never to bring undercover cops to shooting galleries.

I accompanied the lead dealer into the kitchen, where I bought a good amount of dope and got ready to leave. Then the dealer told me: "You're not going anywhere, until you shoot up." Conjuring up an excuse, I explained that I had to get back quickly, to give the dope to others.

The dealer wasn't convinced. "I need to see you shoot up, so I know you're not a cop."

"I don't even have my works with me," I explained.

He brought out a box of new syringes. "Go ahead, pick your own rig."

I looked around the apartment, seeing almost everyone – all black guys, both dealers and users – checking me out to see where this confrontation was going. The other sellers in the place looked to be on edge, getting ready to pounce. I grabbed the lead dealer by the throat, pulling out my .25 automatic, and dragged him over to the window, which I then opened. Next, I grabbed a chair with my free hand and threw it out the window, to alert my backup team to rush in and make the arrests before somebody got shot. The team was around the corner and heard my "alarm". They raced upstairs, pounding on the door. But the door they hit had a Fox lock on the inside: a metal bar, fastened to the inside of the door about two-thirds of the way up on a heavy metal plate, and set back at an angle into a metal bracket on the floor. The backup team pounded on the door, but the Fox lock held strong.

Meanwhile, the other dealers had pulled their guns out, threatening to blow me away. Still holding my guy by the throat, I pressed the .25 to him and told the others "I'll shoot him," and they believed me. After what seemed like an eternity, the Emergency Services Unit, who the team had called in, arrived and battered the door down, rescuing me and completing the bust.

At the time of that bust – previously noted – I lived in an apartment in the basement of a one family house on the other side of Sheepshead Bay, in Manhattan Beach. The Triumph Spitfire I had been driving was parked on the street in front of the house.

Fortunately, I moved away from that Manhattan Beach apartment shortly after the harrowing experience on the fifth floor of that tenement building. A uniformed patrolman named Richard

Jones moved into where I'd been living. It wasn't long before a gang of those that we'd busted some time ago tracked down my whereabouts. The Spitfire may have tipped them off to my location. Anyway, when this group of at least 15 very angry young white men came to find me at the apartment, Patrolman Jones told them that I no longer lived there. Turns out they had been arrested during the Sheepshead Bay operation. Had I been alone there when they came, I'd have been many rounds short of holding them off, to save my life. My concerns were hardly dramatic. Some of these guys didn't give a damn about their own lives. They surely had no regard for mine.

While still with Narcotics, I decided to trade my Spitfire for a different Triumph, a TR6. I went to Nemet Motors, a Triumph dealership in Jamaica, Queens, where I purchased my new car.

When I brought the car in for a 5,000 mile check-up, I asked the people in the service department: "How long will this take ?" I was told that the book calls for 3 hours, as they'd do a thorough initial check, including door locks and other items.

I left my new car with the Nemet's Service Dept. and took a walk up Jamaica Avenue, browsing in stores. Forty five minutes later I returned to the dealership and found my car parked in the corner of the garage. I asked if my car had been serviced and they told me it was ready and handed me an invoice. I looked at the charges, noting a 3-hour labor charge.

"I was only gone for 45 minutes," I protested.

"Well, that's what the book calls for," said the service manager.

"I'm not paying for 3 hours of labor, when you only worked on it for 45 minutes," I told him.

"Then you're not getting your key," he told me, walking away. I took my spare key from the magnetized case on the car's undercarriage and started the car and began pulling out. Shutting the garage door before I got out, the manager shouted: "I'm calling the cops!"

Soon a radio car from the 103rd Precinct came to the dealership and listened to the complaint against me. The cops looked at me and they thought I was a skell, with my long hair, beard and hippie outfit. When the two cops approached me I identified myself.

"Before you start," I told them, "I'm on the job."

I explained that I was an Undercover Narcotics cop, showed them my badge and explained how this shop was trying to rip me off by charging me for 3 hours labor on a 45 minute job.

The responding cops told Nemet's service manager; "Give him his keys. You've got his name and address. You can take him to court, if you want. He's one of us."

I never heard from Nemet Motors again.

The scariest encounter I had happened early in my role in Undercover Narcotics.

The story begins with an UC narcotics cop who was working out of the main UC office in Old Slip, Manhattan. This UC cop bought drugs from another cop who had ties with a major drug dealer named Charlie C. His last name will not be used in this account. When word got to him, Charlie C. wanted to put a contract out on the UC cop, so that the cop who was working with him could get off. The idea was that the criminal cop who'd sold the drugs would beat the rap if there was no one to testify against him.

At the time I was working out of Brooklyn South. They gave me a CI to work with who knew Charlie C. and was able to get me an introduction. We went to where Charlie lived – in a row of brick townhouses, across from the Marlboro Housing Project – within the confines of the 62nd Precinct. The CI introduced me to Charlie C., and I was able to purchase an ounce of heroin – an "A" buy.

This Charlie C. was one mean-looking character, and he was a junkie (heroin addict) to boot. When I wanted to go back to him to make a "B" buy, the CI was petrified of a return and refused to go. So, I asked for another UC to accompany me on a second buy, this time for two ounces of heroin. The UC cop who joined me, also from Brooklyn South was named Steven Spinelli. I was then relatively new to UC Narcotics, but Spinelli had done UC for several years. Prior to police work he'd been a Marine, and worked on the Tactical Patrol Force (TPF) before Narcotics.

Spinelli and I went to meet Charlie C. at his house and found him with another guy. We were told to join them in their car, so we left ours (an unmarked car, with phony license plates) and got into the back seat of their car together. These guys drove to a place called Graves End Bay, at the end of Bay Parkway, across from Coney Island, where they took us to a deserted area and stopped the car.

Suddenly, the two in the front seat turned around to face us, one with a .45 Automatic and the other holding a .357 Magnum Revolver. With the guns pointed right at our faces, Charlie said, "If you're cops, we're gonna kill you."

I totally froze and saw my whole life pass before my eyes in a matter of seconds. I didn't move a muscle, as they'd have blown us away at the slightest twitch. But Spinelli was so cool that we used to say that he "pissed ice."

Spinelli didn't hesitate in his response. "How do I know that you guys aren't cops, looking to rip us off ?"

The two put their guns down and turned around.

Shortly thereafter, we made the buy.

Charlie C. and the other guy were later arrested and went to prison. Besides the drug bust, the success of the operation was that we avoided the UC Charlie wanted a hit put out on from getting killed. That UC from Old Slip rose through the ranks, eventually ascending to 3-Star Chief in the department.

More recently – perhaps 5 or 6 years ago – another incident took place in the very same deserted area of Graves End Bay. Two black New York Police Department Detectives were there, attempting to make a gun buy. Both were found shot dead at that location.

A unique situation arose while I was working undercover. While driving my Spitfire along Eastern Parkway, bearing phony, out-of-state license plates, I was pulled over by uniformed cops in a patrol car from the 77th Precinct.

The officers exited their car, and one of them came up to the driver's window and asked me for ID. With both of my hands on the steering wheel, I replied that I was on the job and had no identification. I then informed him that I was carrying my weapon (a .25 caliber automatic) in my boot.

"Show me your tin," he demanded. To which I told him that I was working Undercover Narcotics, and was on my way to a buy. Still, the officer didn't seem to believe me, indicating that his distrust was based on my failure to have produced anything to validate my story. I then ripped open my shirt, showing them the wire I was wearing for the bust. The two officers ran back to their car and took off, without another word.

A letter dated September 27, 1973 from the Commanding Officer of the Narcotics Division, Robert J. Johnston, Jr, Inspector, Executive Officer, Narcotics Division was sent to the Director of Police Personnel. The subject: REQUEST FOR PERMANENT CADRE STATUS , noting that "Police Officer Rosen … has displayed an outstanding ability and initiative in the performance of his assigned duties, and his integrity is beyond question." This letter was co-signed, as a 1st Endorsement by James Taylor, Chief, Organized Crime Control.

Permanent Cadre status meant that I had earned the privilege of working Narcotics for as long as I chose. Standard procedure was for officers to be assigned to Narcotics for a period of two years.

Meanwhile, someone new had come into my life, forever altering my routine. As a single UC Narcotics cop I worked crazy hours, often late into the night. My social life was restricted to those who also worked similar shifts, so the women I'd dated were usually stewardesses – they weren't referred to as flight attendants then – or nurses.

One night while still working in uniform, after finishing the 4-12 shift at the 79th, I and 4 or 5 other cops decided to go to the Tempo dance club at the Sheraton Hotel at LaGuardia Airport. We arrived at about 12:15 – which was late – as the dance was set to end at 1 o'clock. I saw an attractive young lady with another cop, Ira Gottlieb. Not shy, I asked her to dance and she accepted. I found out that her name was Christine, and after our dance I asked for her phone number. She politely declined, but I was smitten.

I knew that Gottlieb had Christine's phone number, so a few days later I called him to ask him about her. He admitted to having her number, but refused to give it to me. Finally, I told him, "You're not getting anywhere with her. I'll give you the phone numbers to 4 or 5 other girls, any one of whom you'll 'get lucky' with." He agreed, so I had a phone number.

The first time I called Christine I caught her as she was just leaving home, dressed and on her way to Europe. When she returned, we began dating, which we continued for about 5 years.

During much of that time I was working UC. Sometimes that meant that I'd need to disappear for months at a time, a situation Christine grew tired of. When we got engaged in July of 1974 she told me that: 'You can't keep that job." I was hoping to marry the lady the following July, but Christine wanted a February wedding. In November of 1974 I left UC and went to the 67th Detective Squad. We were married by the Police Chaplain, Rabbi Alvin Kass at his temple in Astoria, Queens, in February, 1975, so Christine won out on both counts.

Other factors also influenced my decision to move out of undercover narcotics. The lifestyle and posturing necessary to successfully infiltrate the drug culture required me to acquire different identities. Sometimes I played the role of a low-level drug dealer – other times I assumed the role of a high-level drug dealer. This meant not only changes of appearance, but attitude and language, as well.

One Thanksgiving I accepted an invitation from my father for Thanksgiving dinner at his house. It was at a table full of friends and family who'd gathered to share love and thankfulness that I blurted out for someone to "Pass the fuckin' butter." When everyone looked at me aghast, I realized what I'd done and offered: "Oh, shit!"

My father later pulled me aside, telling me that I had "to get out of there," meaning the undercover narcotics unit. He could see how my role-playing on the job was negatively affecting my personal life. And he was right.

POLICE DEPARTMENT
NEW YORK, N. Y. 10013

August 8, 1973

Daniel P. Horowitz
Deputy Inspector General
Housing and Development Administration
2 Lafayette Street
Room 800
New York, New York   10007

Dear Inspector Horowitz:

Police Commissioner Donald F. Cawley has asked me to acknowledge, with thanks, your recent letter.

It is indeed a pleasure to know that these Officers performed their duty in such a manner as to warrant your commendation.

Your kindness in writing will be brought to the attention of these Officers and their superiors, after which appropriate notation will be made in their personal file as a permanent record.

Sincerely,

Donald F. Cawley
POLICE COMMISSIONER

By: _____
    Deputy Inspector

bcg

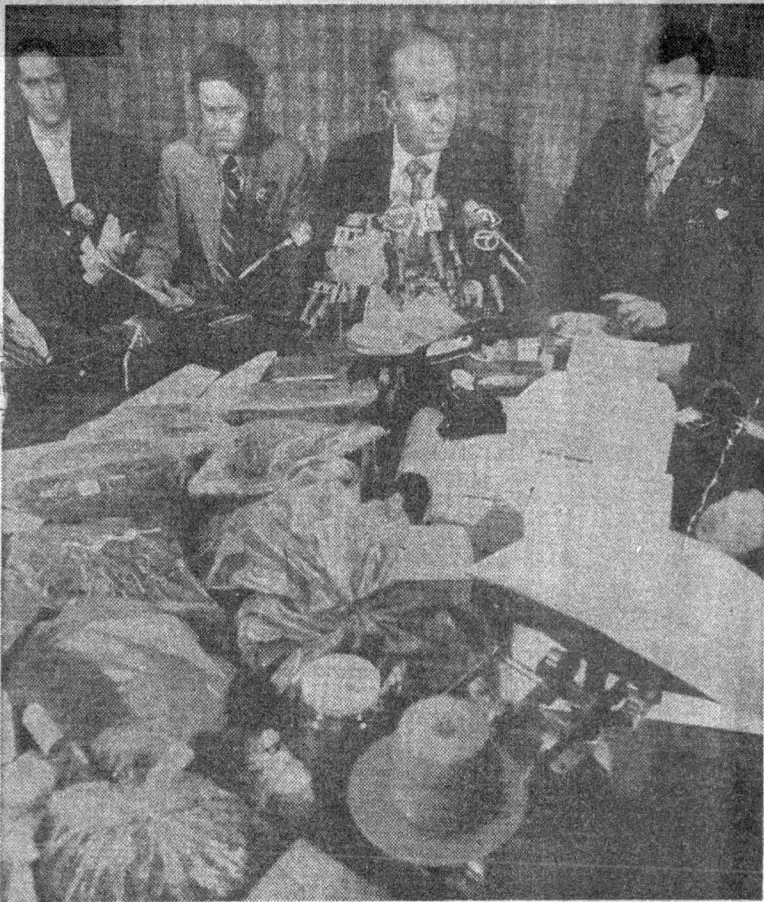

The New York Times

NEW YORK, TUESDAY, FEBRUARY 27, 1973

The New York Times/Lee Romero

Brooklyn District Attorney Eugene Gold, second from right, displaying drugs and paraphernalia seized in overnight raids. With Mr. Gold are law-enforcement officials.

STUDENTS SEIZED IN SALE OF DRUGS

5 High School Pupils Among 21 Held as Pushers at 4 Colleges and Schools

By MORRIS KAPLAN

Five high school students—including two 14-year-old boys—and four college students were among 21 persons arrested yesterday on charges of selling narcotics at two colleges and two schools in Brooklyn.

District Attorney Eugene Gold said the use of drugs was "widespread" in the schools and "a very real problem" on the two campuses, Brooklyn College and Kingsborough Community College. He listed a self-described drug counselor at Brooklyn College and a Transit Authority patrolman as principal suspects.

In an overnight sweep that ended at 3 A.M., detectives seized cocaine, heroin, marijuana, amphetamines, drug paraphernalia and two loaded handguns. They handcuffed the defendants for arraignment in Brooklyn Criminal Court, where arrest warrants had been issued earlier for four fugitives.

Mr. Gold called six of the suspects distributors, and said they funneled the drugs to pushers heading four separate operations. The District Attor-

Continued on Page 44, Column 3

STUDENTS SEIZED IN SALE OF DRUGS

Continued From Page 1, Col. 1

ney said the operations netted almost $500,000 a year from sales to students at Brooklyn College, Kingsborough Community, in the Manhattan Beach section, Midwood High School, which is next to Brooklyn College in the Flatbush section, and Ditmas Junior High School, also in Flatbush.

He identified the self-styled drug counselor as 28-year-old Michael De Castro of 1722 West Fourth Street, in the Gravesend-Bensonhurst section. A part-time psychology student at Brooklyn College, Mr. Castro conducted an encounter-group program and peddled hashish and LSD, according to Mr. Gold.

Mr. De Castro operated out of a trailer parked "in close proximity" to the college campus, he said.

Harold Harris, a spokesman for the college, said the college had not been aware of either the trailer or the suspect's counseling. He described Mr. De Castro as a part-time night student taking one course in psychology.

POLICE DEPARTMENT

NEW YORK, N. Y. 10013

September 27, 1973

From: Commanding Officer, Narcotics Division

To: Director of Police Personnel

Subject: REQUEST FOR PERMANENT CADRE STATUS

1.   Request Permanent Cadre status for the following named Police Officer:

NAME	SHIELD	T.R. #	COMMAND
ROSEN, Gary	13112	865622	Bklyn. South N.D.

2.   Police Officer Rosen was assigned to the Narcotics Division May 10, 1972.

3.   During his tenure he has displayed an outstanding ability and initiative in the performance of his assigned duties, and his integrity is beyond question.

4.   Field Control Division record check failed to disclose anything that would preclude Permanent Cadre status for Police Officer Rosen.

ROBERT J. JOHNSTON, JR.
Inspector
Executive Officer
Narcotics Division

pc

cc: OCCB-Admin., Sgt. Hilsenrath

1ST ENDORSEMENT
Chief, Organized Crime Control to Director of Police Personnel.
September 28, 1973. APPROVED. Forwarded for your information.

JAMES TAYLOR
Chief
Organized Crime Control

pc

POLICE DEPARTMENT

NEW YORK, N.Y. 10013

November 16, 1973

Daniel P. Horowitz
Deputy Inspector General
Housing and Development Administration
2 Lafayette Street
Room 800
New York, New York   10007

Dear Sir:

Police Commissioner Donald F. Cawley
has asked me to acknowledge, with thanks,
your recent letter.

It is indeed a pleasure to know that
these Officers performed their duty in such
a manner as to warrant your commendation.

Your warm expressions will be brought
to the attention of these Officers and their
superiors, after which appropriate notation
will be made in their personal file as a
permanent record.

Sincerely,

Donald F. Cawley
POLICE COMMISSIONER

By: _____
Deputy Inspector

bcg

The City of New York

HOUSING AND DEVELOPMENT ADMINISTRATION
ANDREW P. KERR, *Administrator*

Office of the Inspector General
2 LAFAYETTE STREET, ROOM 800   NEW YORK, N. Y. 10007

LAWRENCE J. DEMPSEY, *Inspector General*

PERSONAL and UNOFFICIAL

December 18, 1973

Hon. Donald F. Cawley
Commissioner
New York City Police Department
1 Police Plaza
New York, N.Y.   10038

Dear Commissioner Cawley:

In my letter to you on November 12, 1973, I inadvertently omitted
the name of Police Officer Gary Rosen whose name should have been included in the second paragraph of my letter.

Once again, I would like to bring to your attention the fine work
performed by members of your Department.

For your information, I am enclosing a Xerox copy of my letter of
November 12, 1973.

Very truly yours,

Daniel P. Horowitz
Deputy Inspector General, HDA

DPH/ls
Enc.

Part Three
White Shield

POLICE DEPARTMENT

NEW YORK, N.Y. 10038

Pct. 426

June 25, 1976

Mrs. Ann E. Hagan
540 East 43 Street
Brooklyn, New York

Dear Mrs. Hagan:

We are in receipt of your most welcome letter
commending the following officers of this
command:

    P.O. Gary Rosen, shield #13112, 67 P.I.U.
    Det. Edward Samuelsen, shield #148, 67 P.I.U.
    Det. Paul Riley, shield #1117, 67 P.I.U.
    P.O. Robert Noblin, shield #24153, 67 Pct.
    P.O. James Geissler, shield #28932, 67 Pct.

Personally, and on behalf of the officers who
have been informed of same, I would like to take
this opportunity to thank you for your kind
expression of appreciation.

Kenneth Fichtelman
Captain

re/

Chapter Seven

Effective November 12, 1974, I went from the Narcotics Division to the Detective Squad of the 67th Precinct. Those of us who had not yet been promoted to the rank of Gold Shield Detective were referred to as White Shield Detectives. Due to the city's fiscal hardships, all promotions were on hold at this time.

All the Precinct Detective Squads had been taken out of the Detective Bureau and placed into the Patrol Bureau, identified as P.I.U. (Precinct Investigation Units). The units worked under the Commanding Officer of each precinct the detectives were working from. We still identified ourselves as Detective Squads, but because we were working out of the Patrol Bureau, they referred to us as PIU.

The average guy in the Detective Squad was 10 years older than I at that time. Most were married; with children, and I was still very young and single.

As a newly-arrived member, one of the first encounters I had with others at the 67th Precinct was when I was approached in the squad room of the second floor by a uniformed officer.

"Are you Gary Rosen?," asked the guy.

I thought to myself, "Who the fuck did I piss off, now ?" I confirmed that I was Gary Rosen.

At this time he told me that his name was Bill Creelman, and that his reason for seeking me out was to welcome me to the 67, so we shook hands.

I was reassigned to uniformed patrol duty for a brief period (less than a month) in 1975. This was because the city's fiscal difficulties had forced the department to lay off 5,000 police officers, so some of us White Shield Detectives assumed their duties temporarily.

In uniform, I was assigned to the 5th Precinct in Chinatown. On weekends we were sent to work our shift in the 6th Precinct in Greenwich Village. One case I worked on there was a bribery arrest in August of 1975. On night duty with Officer Arthur Williams and me in uniform, we were given the Washington Square Park detail in lower Manhattan. Observing a dice game near the fountain circle in the park, we approached and all the participants scattered, except for James Baldwin, a 36 year old who lived adjacent to the park on Washington Place. Mr. Baldwin offered us $12.50 to allow the game to continue. We took the money, but told him that we would need to confer with our supervisor. So, we took him to the 6th Precinct station house where we notified Sergeant Bernard Kelly, the station house supervisor. After Sergeant Kelly informed I.A.D. (Internal Affairs Division) of the situation, an I.A.D. Sergeant came over and "wired me" with an electronic recording device. Next Kelly, Williams and I engaged Baldwin in further conversation about his suggested arrangements with me wearing the wire. Baldwin then gave Kelly $6 and offered the three of us $50 each, weekly, to allow his game to run unhampered by the police. He also offered to inform on two other persons who were operating dice games in Washington Square Park.

At this point, Baldwin was placed under arrest for bribery and he was informed of his rights.

After 2,000 of the 5,000 patrolmen who had been laid off were brought back, I shirked the uniform, went back to the 67th Detective Squad and had to perform uniformed duty only one more time.

The Detective Squad at the 67th was under the Precinct Commanding Officer. I was informed by the Administrative Lieutenant Bradley that I was assigned to a parade detail, in uniform, along 5th Avenue in Manhattan. I tried to get out of it, protesting that my shoulder length long hair wouldn't look appropriate in a uniformed parade rank.

"Don't assign me to this."

The Lieutenant simply replied, "That's an order."

So I had no choice.

Driving from Brooklyn into Manhattan in my Triumph TR6 (in full uniform) I could see how packed the streets already were, so I parked on 1st Avenue and began walking toward 5th Ave. A radio car pulled up to me, and from the passenger side the window rolled down and a New York City Police Captain from Traffic Unit Safety B said, "Officer, I didn't know the circus was in town."

"Captain, I don't know, I'm not from this precinct. I don't know where the circus is. I was detailed to parade duty," I replied

"No. You're the circus. You shouldn't be in uniform, with that hair."

He threatened to "write me up" so I had to think fast.

"My uncle told me I had to come."

"Who's your uncle ?" the captain asked.

"Chief Sidney Cooper," I replied.

The captain rolled up his window, and the car took off.

At that time, Sidney Cooper was the Chief of I.A.D. (Internal Affairs Division), and nobody – including the captain that was busting my balls – wanted anything to do with Chief Cooper. I had never met or spoken to Chief Cooper in my life. He was the most disliked man in the police department.

By the time I got to 5th Avenue, the parade was ready to go. I reported to the Lieutenant in charge of Ceremonial Unit who was pissed at me for being 15 minutes late. I told him that I'd been stopped by a captain who'd threatened to give me a write-up because of my long hair. When he asked which captain, I described the captain to him saying he was from Traffic Unit Safety B and he said, "Him? He's a scumbag!" There were 3 officers holding flags at the front of the parade detail. The Lieutenant went up to one of the officers, and told him to give me his flag. So, I was now in the lead with the two other officers, carrying flags.

~

During my first five years with the New York City Police Department, I had acquired an impressive arrest record, and was known to have had a penchant for tough assignments. I had now shaven my beard, but retained the long hair and earing – the better to blend in when operating as a plainclothes cop in the mid-70s New York scene. I was the only Jewish undercover cop in Brooklyn South.

New York had some 32,000 men and women in the police department then, not including civilian personnel. When I came on the Force, only 3000 of them were Jewish – just under 10% of the entire department. Bruce Felton, in a story in the *Times of Israel* and *World Jewish Review*, noted Jewish representation on the Force. Concurrent with the city's drive to include black, Hispanic and other minorities on the force, there was an effort to recruit more Jews to police work as well, assisted by The Shomrim Society. The goal was to make the Department more responsive to the diverse ethnic makeup of the city. Previously, when the Department announced an exam, those who responded were overwhelmingly Irish or Italian.

Exceptions were Jewish police in ranking capacities. In fact, 2 of 3 Jews on the force were above the rank of patrolman. This included Detectives, Sergeants, Lieutenants, and Captains. During the early 70s, one out of every three Captains was a Jew. The rank of Captain was the highest civil service rank. Above that, these were political appointments. These political appointments included: Deputy Inspector, Inspector, Deputy Chief (1 Star), Assistant Chief (2 Stars), Chiefs of various bureaus (3 Stars), Chief Inspector (4 Stars). Many of the early ranking officers were Depression babies, who became WWII veterans. They had graduated college, and were familiar with the discipline and study habits needed to pass civil service examinations to receive higher departmental ranks. A notable Jew at that time was Sanford Garilek, who became the first Jewish Chief Inspector. Probably the most famous Jewish Chief was Al Siedman, Chief of Detectives. Howard Safir became the first Jewish Police Commissioner of New York City.

In the history of the New York City Police Department women were unable to obtain rank, as they'd not been permitted to even apply for positions of rank. Women cops sued the city and won, and were finally offered applications for the Sergeants' exam.

The first female promoted to the rank of Sergeant was Felicia Spritzer who later became a Lieutenant, happened to be

Jewish. Another Jewish woman, Gertrude Schimmel was quite exceptional. She passed the exams necessary and became Sergeant, then Lieutenant, then Captain. By way of political appointment she received the further ranks of Deputy Inspector, Inspector and then Deputy Chief Inspector (1 Star), becoming the first woman promoted to that position, and the highest ranking female in the entire Department.

Some found it ironic that when I was doing undercover work, I took part in roughly 300 drug busts: At least 250 of them involved Jewish pushers. I referred to them as "scum", as they were selling poison. At times, it proved easier for me to infiltrate with them, as we had common ethnic backgrounds.

~

As part of my continuing education, I attended a Basic Criminal Investigation course at John Jay College of Criminal Justice, and received a certificate of completion on June 18, 1976. This was part of the Summer Workshop Program jointly sponsored by the Criminal Justice Center and the Pinkerton Foundation. These programs were developed to offer courses which had practical applications and served the law enforcement community.

In fact, I signed up for and took every investigative course the police department offered. I successfully completed all the classes I enrolled in, including courses in Homicide Investigation, Sex Crimes, and Criminal Investigation. Unfortunately, the courses at the F.B.I. Academy weren't available to me, because only police at the rank of Lieutenant or above were eligible to enroll.

~

There was a case that took place in the mid-1970s, when three individuals were arrested for bilking the New York State Department of Labor out of more than $50,000 in fraudulent unemployment insurance claims, over the span of two years. The three – all women – were Mrs. Maria Diraimondo (51) of Staten Island, Mrs. Rose Ruva (61) of Brooklyn, and her sister Mrs. Ada Messina (53), with the same Brooklyn address. They were charged with grand larceny and forgery. Using different names, with Mrs. Messina as employer reference, they received unearned, undeserved unemployment insurance funds netting Mrs. Ruva $900, Mrs. Diraimondo $22,000 and Mrs. Messina $28,000.

In addition, Mrs. Ruva and her sister, Mrs. Messina, an attorney, were additionally charged with fraudulent claims to homeowners insurance companies. The two women had alleged home burglaries and the theft of their luggage while on vacation claiming $24,000 in losses. The two allegedly collected $11,000. Because this case became so complex, I requested the assistance of the New York State Attorney General's Office for matters regarding unemployment and Workman's Comp. I also sought assistance from the U.S. Postal Inspectors, as the frauds were conducted through the mail and requested help from the Internal Revenue Service, because the fraudulent operations used phony corporations, which were set up with Federal Employment Identification Numbers. Working closely with Geico Insurance Company, we documented and proved many of the fraudulent insurance claims the perpetrators had filed. I also worked with Sears and Roebuck, as the women had purchased a great deal of furniture and appliances fraudulently from them.

I arrested the perpetrators and they were prosecuted by the Brooklyn District Attorney's Office.

The accused lawyer, Mrs. Messina was arrested again about a year later, this time indicted by the Federal Government for violation of the Federal Statutes that I uncovered during our investigation. These federal charges were brought by the U.S. Postal Inspectors and the Internal Revenue Service.

My work on these cases for the 67th Squad included many months of investigative accumulation of information. The charts I composed on oak tag stock became difficult to decipher, with all of Messina's activities marked in criss-crossing graphics across the board. In addition to her using fraudulent credit cards to buy appliances and furniture from Sears, she had even gone so far as to attempt to sell a supposed manuscript which had been written by Christopher Columbus for a million dollars.

Ironically, during the initial arrest, Mrs. Messina's first name was listed in all capitals. Her name appeared as "ADA Messina", which confused those at the prosecutor's office, who put her indictment aside (thinking her name referred to Assistant District Attorney), until our subsequent investigation uncovered the typographical error and finally held her accountable.

~

On April 30, 1975 Thomas A. Sullivan, Supervisor of the 67th Detective Squad wrote to the Commanding Officer of the 67th Precinct formally, offering a 1st Endorsement, which "requests that consideration be given to advancing Police Officer Gary Rosen, shield # 13112 to the rank of Detective Investigator." This meant that Sullivan was endorsing my elevation to the rank of a Gold Shield Detective for first time, with me being assigned to the Detective Squad. However, I had previously been recommended three other times for a Gold Shield, while working undercover.

At that stage I'd already earned Departmental Recognition in the category of four (4) Meritorious Police Duty and four (4) Excellent Police Duty, with no complaints. My "prompt and thorough" investigations required little supervision to accomplish tasks assigned to me.

Unfortunately, New York City – and by extension the NYC Police Dept. – were under severe fiscal difficulties. My Gold Shield would have to wait.

~

The 67th Detective Squad was headed by the Squad Commander Sergeant Thomas Sullivan. Within the squad were 3 teams of Detectives, with 2-3 men in each team. A team would work 2 shifts from 4 pm - 1 am, then 2 shifts from 8 am – 4 pm, and then would be off for 56 hours. There was also a Night Watch, working 1 shift from 4 pm – 8 am, then 1 shift from midnight – 8 am, which gave you some extra time off. Occasionally, one detective from one of the teams covered the Night Watch, meaning that he'd be working in a Night Watch Team which consisted of detectives from other squads. It was also possible that one of the regular teams might be forced to operate a shift with only one detective. In fact, many times a detective would be working by himself, for various reasons: night watch, vacation, sick leave, court appearances, etc.

There was a case in the 67th when I found myself alone. The Detective Squad on this case worked under the Precinct Captain (who was part of the Patrol Bureau, not the Detective Bureau), as this was a burglary of less than $5000. Burglaries in excess of $5000 went to the Burglary Squad. I was assigned, along with two uniformed cops. We were told that the perpetrators were expected to return to the scene to take more items from this apartment, and we were sent there to await their arrival. The two uniforms accompanying me came to the apartment, but only stayed a short time. They decided that they were going to leave and go to the movies, taking the only police radio with them.

After they left, I was still at the apartment alone in the dark, when a group of five young black men came in through a window which had been broken during the previous burglary. I identified myself and had my handgun pulled, ordering them against the wall. Now I had my hands full. In the room with me were these five guys who'd do practically anything to avoid arrest, and I was in a locked apartment with them by myself, without the radio that the two uniformed patrolmen had taken with them. This was way before there were cell phones, so – still holding my gun on these guys – I opened the apartment's door and began to holler down the hall for someone to call 911, again identifying myself as a policeman. Someone did call. I was rescued by fellow officers, and I arrested all the perpetrators. The first cop to arrive at the scene was Officer Bill Creelman.

Thereafter, whenever I found myself working alone and was going to make an arrest, I'd go to the Desk Officer on duty at the 67th and ask if Officer Bill Creelman was working that day. If he was, I'd take him with me as backup. He was a real good cop, reliable and trustworthy. When situations became heated and we had to mix it up physically with dangerous criminals, Bill was the man to have beside me. He and I have remained close friends since 1974.

Gary Rosen serving parade detail
5th Avenue, Manhattan

POLICE DEPARTMENT
CITY OF NEW YORK

April 30, 1975 APS#661

From: Supervisor, 67 Precinct Investigating Unit

To: Commanding Officer, 67 Precinct

Subject: RECOMMENDATION FOR ADVANCEMENT TO DETECTIVE INVESTIGATOR
            FOR POLICE OFFICER GARY ROSEN, SHIELD #13112, 67 P.I.U.

1.   The undersigned requests that consideration be given
to advancing Police Officer Gary Rosen, shield #13112, tax registry
#865622, to the rank of Detective Investigator.

2.   Police Officer Gary Rosen was appointed to the Department on July 15, 1971. The Officer holds Departmental Recognition
in the category of four (4) Meritorious Police Duty and four (4)
Excellent Police Duty, and no complaints. The assignments of the
Officer are as follows:

        July 15, 1971 to September 6, 1971 Recruit Training
        September 7, 1971 to February 25, 1972 Patrol, 79 Precinct
        February 26, 1972 to November 12, 1974 Undercover
        Narcotics, Brooklyn South Area
        November 13, 1974 to present Investigations, 67 P.I.U.

3.   While assigned to this Unit, the Officer has been
observed by the undersigned and found to be a competent investigator.
The Officer handles investigations promptly and thoroughly, with
little supervision required to accomplish the task. The reports
submitted by the Officer are succinct and always prompt. This
Officer is an asset to the Department and worthy of advancement to
the rank of Detective Investigator.

4.   For your information and necessary attention.

                                    Thomas F. Sullivan
                                    Thomas F. Sullivan
                                    Supervisor, 67 Detectives

TFS/bg

1st ENDORSEMENT

From: Commanding Officer, 67 Precinct To: Commanding Officer,
Brooklyn South Area   May 8, 1975. The undersigned concurs with
the evaluation and recommendation of Sergeant Sullivan. Recommend
advancement to the rank of Detective Investigator.

                                    Kenneth Fichtelman
                                    Captain, 67 Precinct

Misc. 243 (Rev. 3-74)

CIVILIAN COMPLAINT REVIEW BOARD
POLICE DEPARTMENT, CITY OF NEW YORK

200 PARK AVENUE SOUTH   at 17th STREET
NEW YORK, N. Y. 10003   •   TELEPHONE 673-6001

MEMBERS OF THE BOARD
ABRAHAM P. CHESS, *Chairman*

ROOSEVELT DUNNING
A. BERNARD KELLAND
FRANCIS B. LOONEY
LUIS M. NECO

WILLIAM T. JOHNSON
Executive Director

GEORGE J. RIOS
Deputy Director

EDWARD C. CIFFONE
Deputy Director

May 2, 1974

RE: CCRB NO. 230 (74)

Dear Officer:

A complaint made against you at the Civilian Complaint Review Board and in connection with which you were interviewed, was referred for conciliation and informal settlement.

Please be advised that this matter has been informally settled through the conciliation procedure. The Review Board has recommended to the Police Commissioner that this matter be concluded as having been settled and the Police Commissioner has approved that recommendation.

Pursuant to the provisions of Charter 21, Rules and Procedures, New York City Police Department, the fact of this complaint is confidential and no notation of any kind shall be made in your personal record folder on file with the Department.

Thank you for your cooperation in this matter.

Very truly yours,

William T. Johnson
Executive Director
Civilian Complaint
Review Board

WTJ/mw

POLICE DEPARTMENT
NEW YORK, N.Y. 10038

Report Under

P.G.   110-50

August 3,1975

From: Captain Peter DeLuca, 6th Precinct

To   :

Subject: BRIBERY ARREST BY POLICE OFFICER

   1. At 2325 hrs.,this date P.O.Gary Rosen, Shield #13112 5th Pct.
while on duty in uniform arrested James Baldwin M-B-36yrs.,79 Washington Pl.,Rm.210,for Bribery 200P.L. and promoting gambling.

   2. The arrest took place in the Sixth Precinct station house
under the following circumstances:

     a) At 2100 hrs. P.O.Rosen and P.O.Arthur Williams Sh.#39128
5th Precinct,assigned to Washington Square Park detail, observed a
dice game near the fountain circle in the park. As the officers
approached all the participants scattered except Baldwin who offered
the officers $12.50 to allow the game to go on . The officers took
the money but told Baldwin they would have to confer with their
supervisor and accompanied him to the 6th Precinct where they
notified Sgt.Bernard Kelly Sh.#2788, station house supervisor.

     b) Sgt.Kelly then informed I.A.D. of the situation.IAD#205
As a result of this notification,P.C.Larence Conner Sh.#28862 IAD
responded to the 6th Precinct and wired P.O.Rosen with an electric
recording device.

     c) Sgt.Kelly with Officers Rosen and Williams then engaged
Baldwin in a conversation during the corse of which Baldwin gave
Sgt.Kelly $6.00 and offered the three officers the sum of $50.00
each weekly to allow his game to run unhampered by the police.
In addition, Baldwin offered to inform on two other persons who
were operating dice games in Washington Square Park.

     d) At this point, Baldwin was placed under arrest and
informed of his rights.

DETECTIVE - INVESTIGATOR

Effective 0001, November 12, 1974.

Ernest P. Libasci, 855871, from 28th Precinct (I.U.) to 113th Precinct (I.U.).

POLICE OFFICERS

Effective 1130, October 25, 1974.

Hoyt T. Tanner, 855066, from 17th Precinct to Identification Section. NOTE: Police Officer Tanner was placed on MODIFIED ASSIGNMENT, effective 0900, October 24, 1974.

Effective 0001, November 5, 1974.

From Commands indicated to Court Division, Arrest Processing Section.

		From Com'd.
Sandra E. Stout	866907	66 Pct.
Georgianna D. Risch	868402	83 Pct.
Elizabeth A. Zartman	859734	Mil. & Ext.Lv.Desk (P.S.D.)

Joan R. Walther, 862645, from Military & Extended Leave Desk (P.S.D.) to Court Division, Arrest Processing Section. Maternity Leave of Absence, Without Pay, terminated effective 0900, November 4, 1974. Twenty-seven days to be deducted from 1974 vacation and three days from 1975 vacation.

Effective 0001, November 12, 1974.

From Narcotics Division (O.C.C.B.) to Precinct Investigation Units specified.

		To Pct. (I.U.)
Joseph A. Petruso	859996	7
Frank X. Viggiano	858864	M-T No.
William M. O'Hara	841462	28
Gary M. Rosen	865622	67
Mack A. Ferguson	861240	71
Joseph R. Edelmann	857663	79
William R. Crowe	857600	88
Harold V. Paulson	852104	94
Robert J. Sasso	856042	104

Chapter Eight

1976 was a year when there was a spike in attacks on the elderly – almost exclusively by young men. At this time I was working with the 70th Detective Squad.

One such incident was the holdup of a senior citizen partner in a prominent investment securities firm. Nathan A. Krumholz of Wechsler & Krumholz, Inc. returned home at 5pm to his apartment house at 650 Ocean Avenue in Brooklyn on November 5th. A man threatened Mr. Krumholz at knife-point and robbed him of $180.

Detective William McLean and I worked the case together, and were able to determine that the person responsible was Donald Carter, whom we arrested. Carter signed a confession and was identified by the victim. I accompanied Mr. Krumholz to the Criminal Court building in Brooklyn on November 8th, where he swore out a complaint and appeared before a Grand Jury, who handed down an indictment the following day.

On November 12, 1976 Mr. Krumholz sent a letter on his firm's letterhead to Police Commissioner Michael J. Codd, thanking the police department, noting that "All citizens can be proud that New York's finest is truly the finest." He mentioned my name a number of times in his letter, explaining that "The expertise and courtesy of Sgt. Terrance Randell (in charge of Detectives, 70th Pct.) and especially Detectives William McLean and Gary Rosen, was a source of comfort."

Within this very same week other attacks on the elderly were taking place. A decoy police officer-disguised as an elderly man, was attacked by a gang of about 15 youths at the foot of the elevated BMT subway station at the corner of Sutphin Blvd. and Jamaica Ave. The youths came running down the subway stairs, crowding around the decoy cop. One of them smashed him on the head with a quart beer bottle, knocking him to the ground. They stole his wallet and tried to remove his wrist watch, when the decoy's backup team raced in to rescue him.

Two of the gang members were arrested for assault and robbery. Judge Melvin Glass sent Melville Dexter (20) of Brooklyn on $25,000 bail, and Fharill Crayton (18) of Manhattan on $5000 bail to Riker's Island. Total amount in the stolen wallet: $1.

Assaults on the elderly were occurring on a daily basis in the city, placing our most vulnerable citizens, men and women at risk, often of losing their lives. The attackers used various weapons in these attacks, including knives and hand guns.

During the 1970s there were a number of incidents in New York with Hasidic Jews that gained nationwide notoriety.

One day, as I was working alone on an investigation for the 70th Squad, a "10-13' call (Officer Needs Assistance) came over the police radio from the 66th Precinct Station House, which was under attack. I responded immediately, as did cops from every borough in the city. As I raced toward the 66th, the entire area was flooded with people on the streets, so I was forced to park a couple of blocks away. Continuing on foot, I saw a mass of 3000 Hasidim pushing toward the precinct, some of whom had already breached the doors of the station house. The image before my eyes looked like a hat commercial in that sea of black garb.

Approaching the mass descending upon the 66th, I managed to gain entrance through a back door. Inside was a scene of pandemonium. A black patrolman had his badge ripped off his uniform, as the Hasidim inside were throwing police files, shouting at the police officers, calling them "Nazi bastards." The attack on the precinct was prompted by the murder of a Hasidic Jew.

After we were able, with much effort to quell the storm, a team was put together to investigate the crimes committed. This team was headed by 2-Star Assistant Chief Mickey Schwartz, the Commanding Officer of all uniformed police in Brooklyn South. Also on the team were: (Jewish) Inspector Levitan, (Jewish) Deputy Inspector Benjamin Hellman, (Jewish) Captain Saul Roseman, (Jewish) Detective Stewart Michaels, from the 66th Detective Squad (which had been assaulted), and me (Jewish, too). Rounding out the team were non-Jews at the levels of: Deputy Inspector, Lieutenant, several Sergeants and other Detectives.

Over the years many units were given abbreviations, or acronyms. For example: S.C.R.U., for Senior Citizens Robbery Unit, T.P.F., for Tactical Patrol Force, S.E.S., for Special Events Squad, and BOSSI, for Bureau of Special Services and Investigations, later referred to as the Intelligence Division. I came up with an acronym for our investigative team: S.H.I.T., for Special Hasidim Investigative Team. We liked the sound of it, but I knew that I'd encounter some problems with that tag at some point.

Our job was to put together a report to identify and bring to justice the persons responsible for assaulting the cops and destroying the precinct during the riot. Following the conclusion of our investigation and making arrests of a number of individuals identified, we took the case to trial.

Although the defense team of the arrested Hasidim tried, they were unable to make a convincing case that the New York City Police Department and – by extension – our investigation, were Anti-Semitic, as most of our team consisted of Jewish policemen.

When I was on the stand testifying, one of the defense attorneys asked me, "Have you ever heard of the term SHIT?"

I sheepishly responded, "Do you mean when you go to the bathroom and move your bowels?"

The defense lawyer said, "No. I'm referring to the term used during the time your unit investigated this case."

"Never heard the term, sir," I responded.

All the defendants copped a plea, except for one who was an attorney himself. He was able to convince the jury that the guilty party wasn't him.

Those charged were found guilty,

The Police Commissioner McGuire (a former U.S. Attorney, whose father was a NYC cop) personally thanked our entire team for the work we'd done on this case. He'd invited us all to his office, and photographs were taken of us with the Commissioner.

Not long after the fiasco at the 66th Precinct, still working out of the 70th, I was driving down Ocean Parkway in an unmarked car when I saw that some young rookie cops had pulled over a car full of Hasidim to the side of the road. These cops were new to the N.S.U., or Neighborhood Stabilization Unit. They'd stopped the car for a traffic infraction and were apparently receiving no cooperation from those in the car. The driver of the car had reportedly been giving the N.S.U. patrolmen a hard time, refusing to hand over his license and calling the cops "Nazis."

I went up to the driver's side of the car and asked the driver for his license and registration. He looked at me and said: "Go fuck yourself." I reached into the car, grabbed him by his long beard, and hauled him out of the car through the open window. He eventually produced his license, and was issued citations by the uniformed patrolmen on the scene.

Some time later, the guy filed a complaint of Anti-Semitism, and I was called before the C.C.R.B. (Civilian Complaint Review Board). In the complaint they listed my last name as Rosa, not Rosen. When the case was reviewed it was determined that I couldn't have been Anti-Semitic, as I was Jewish myself, so I never had to testify and the case went away.

About a half hour before midnight on May 12, 1977, Fordham University sophomore Ernest McCain halted his evening bicycle ride through Brooklyn's Prospect Park. What the young man found literally stopped him in his tracks: The remains of a young male body were floating in the pool of an unoccupied polar bear cage. McCain called police to report his discovery.

I and Detective Joseph Tepedino, also of the 70th Detective Squad, were assigned to investigate the death of this victim, estimated to be about 25 years old. We saw that there were two polar bears in the adjoining cage who expressed interest in our investigation, but they offered no testimony as to what had happened to the young man we found in the pool.

There was speculation that the man may have been climbing the fence which separated the polar bear's cage from the empty cage, when one or both of the bears clawed at the victim, causing him to fall back into the moat of the empty cage. The cage was made of tall iron rods which curved inward at their tops. The rods were reinforced with three horizontal tracks of iron, along the bottom, middle and at the top of the fence's height, just beneath the prongs curving into the cage. Larger vertical iron posts were positioned at 8 foot intervals. Climbing such a cage successfully would be difficult for a human being – bordering on impossible. Tepedino and I wondered how this man had ended up where his remains were found.

This was a bizarre, gruesome scene. We found blood on the cage's fence, a torn shirt draped over it's top, and a pair of brown shoes in a nearby lion's cage. The victim seemed to have been eaten alive by the polar bears, with the bloody remnants of leg muscles evident on massive expanses of exposed bone. Large chunks of flesh were missing: half his face was gone, as was much of his stomach.

When we interviewed the park's Senior Zookeeper, Frank Blomquist, he noted that the empty cage was sometimes used as a nursery for polar bear cubs, to separate them from their mothers. But he'd never come across an unauthorized human in any of the cages.

Unfortunately, this was a case at that time was unsolvable.

But, the story doesn't end there. When I retired to Florida I purchased Louis Eppolito's autobiographical story, Mafia Cop. According to Detective Lou Eppolito's account, he attests that a "badge abuser... who had somehow slipped past the Department's psychological screeners" was responsible for the mutilated body we found at Prospect Park. According to his account, "One of the best investigators I knew in the Seven-One, was a nuclear bomb waiting to explode." Eppolito told of how "The plainclothes officer, off duty, pulled his car over in the [Prospect] park when his tire went flat. Two muggers approached. He collared one and gave him a choice: a bullet in the head or the polar bear cage."

CRIMINAL JUSTICE CENTER
448 west 56th street, ny., ny. 10019
(212) 247-1600-1

June 30, 1976

Sgt. Thomas Sullivan
67 Precinct Investigations Unit
New York City Police Department
2820 Snyder Avenue
Brooklyn, New York

Dear Sgt. Sullivan,

I am most pleased to forward a copy of the certificate received by   Gary Rosen   , who attended the Criminal Justice Center's Summer Workshop Program. We trust that his attendance will be of value to the Department.

The Summer Workshop Program, which was jointly sponsored by the Criminal Justice Center and the Pinkerton Foundation, is designed to offer courses which will have practical application and serve the law enforcement community.

Be assured that we will continue to develop programs designed to assist you and members of your Department. If you are interested in specific areas or courses which you feel may be of value, please don't hesitate to contact me.

Sincerely,

Robert J. McCormack
Executive Director
Criminal Justice Center

Encl:1

john jay college of criminal justice

Criminal Justice Center
John Jay College of Criminal Justice

This is to certify that

GARY ROSEN

has completed the course

Basic Criminal Investigation

offered by the Criminal Justice Center

President

Vice President

Director

JOHN JAY COLLEGE OF CRIMINAL JUSTICE · FOUNDED 1964

Dated _June 18, 1976_

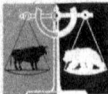

WECHSLER & KRUMHOLZ, INC.
INVESTMENT SECURITIES / 39 BROADWAY, NEW YORK, N.Y. 10006

OVER - THE - COUNTER
CONVERTIBLE BONDS

Detective Gary Rosen
Police Department, City of New York
70th Precinct
154 Lawrence Avenue,
Brooklyn, New York 11201

WECHSLER & KRUMHOLZ, INC.

INVESTMENT SECURITIES / 39 BROADWAY, NEW YORK, N.Y. 10006

TELEPHONE (212) 422-5865 • TELETYPE 212-571-1175

November 12, 1976

Dear Gary:

Hope this describes the entire situation to your satisfaction, and
that it does you some good.

Sincerely,

Nat

WECHSLER & KRUMHOLZ, INC.

INVESTMENT SECURITIES / 39 BROADWAY, NEW YORK, N.Y. 10006

TELEPHONE (212) 422-5865 • TELETYPE 212-571-1175

November 12, 1976

Commissioner Michael J. Codd
Police Dept., City of New York
1 Police Plaza
New York, N.Y. 10013

Dear Commissioner Codd·

In spite of all the criticism directed at your department, my recent experience belies all the poor impressions the public reads and hears of the New York City Police Department.

I am a senior citizen and was held up on Wednesday November 3rd at 5:00 P.M in the lobby of my apartment house at 650 Ocean Avenue, Brooklyn, N.Y. The holdup man threatened me at knife point and forced me to hand over $180.00. This certainly was an unhappy and disturbing experience.

On Saturday, November 6th, the detectives after a great deal of expert work were able to determine that this person was Donald Carter, and on that day arrested him and got a signed confession, and later I identified him. On Monday, November 8th together with Det. Gary Rosen I went to the Criminal Court in Brooklyn, at which time I swore out a complaint and appeared before the Grand Jury, and within a few hours I was able to complete my participation due to the efforts of Det. Rosen. The following day Tuesday, November 9th, the Grand Jury handed down an indictment.

The expertise and courtesy of Sgt. Terrance Randall (in charge of Detectives,70th Pct.) and especially Detectives William McLean and Gary Rosen, was a source of comfort.

All Citizens can be proud that New York's finest is truly the finest.

Cordially,

Nathan A. Krumholz.

NAK:al

Chapter Nine

One Brooklyn case I was involved with centered on an immigrant family named Gini. The head of the family, Miftar Gini was the Superintendent of a building at 533 East Second Street in the Ocean Parkway section of the borough, where the residents were predominantly Puerto Rican. He and his family had fled to America a decade earlier from Albania.

Mr. Gini registered a complaint against someone named Steven Pagan and others for harassment, and I was assigned to investigate. When I went to interview Gini, he told me that he'd been a Lieutenant in the Albanian Secret Police.

"I'm a brother officer." He seemed to be seeking special consideration from me and the department.

I thought to myself, "He was in the Secret Police of an Eastern European Communist regime, I have nothing in common with this guy."

I had, in fact, arrested Pagan on a charge of attempted murder and possession of a weapon, several months earlier. In that investigation, I confirmed that the victim in that case was a relative of Pagan's, who dropped the charges.

On September 8, 1977 Miftar Gini was arrested for the murder of this same 24-year-old Steven Pagan on the street in front of Gini's house.

The Gini defense team offered an explanation for the killing of Pagan, with testimony from Miftar himself, Miftar's wife Dashurije, and daughter Manushaqe. Their story told of an attempted break-in of their apartment from the fire escape outside their fourth floor window. According to them, with the burglary foiled, Miftar rushed to the street and accosted 3 men, one of whom "jabbed at him with a long screwdriver." Pagan was reportedly one of the three men. The N.Y.C. police were alerted, but the 3 men had already fled when they arrived. The family testified that on numerous occasions subsequent to the attempted break-in, Mr. Pagan confronted family members on the street in their neighborhood, threatening to kill them all.

During the trial, Gini's defense attorney asked me if I had given Gini permission to kill Pagan. I testified that I had told Gini that if Pagan continues to harass him, he should call the police and to look to protect his family.

Pagan was shot by Miftar Gini with an illegal gun, which Gini testified that he'd bought to protect his family. Gini stated that he saw Pagan on the street on the day of the shooting, and that Pagan had come at him with a steel window grate, which Pagan thrust at Gini's throat. Gini claimed that he was afraid for his life.

However, two eyewitnesses testified at the trial that they were passing at the time of this deadly encounter. Both witnesses swore that Pagan had no weapon of any sort, and that his empty hands were raised, as he began pleading for his life, "Please God, don't shoot me."

Gini shot Pagan twice. Then, with Pagan crawling through the garbage of an overturned can, seeking anything with which to defend himself, Gini shot the dying man twice more.

After Gini's arrest, Dashurije, Miftar's wife came to visit him up in the squad room. She was carrying a purse which I ordered her to hand over to me. Inside was a handgun. Upon finding the gun, I arrested her for possession of a weapon. The Ballistics Unit soon confirmed that it was the same gun that was used in the murder of Pagan. Mrs. Gini pleaded guilty to the charge against her, and was given a year's probation.

In a November 27, 1978 letter to New York City Police Commissioner Robert McGuire, from Joseph W. Beres, Jr., Chief of Police of Norwalk, Connecticut, it was noted that we at the 70th

Squad had "developed information that one, Carmello Navarro, had fled from our (Norwalk) jurisdiction to the Coney Island section of Brooklyn, New York." Navarro had been sought for a shotgun murder and three (3) counts of Assault With Intent to Commit Murder: two (2) by shotgun and one (1) by knife in Connecticut.

Sergeant William Battista, Detective Paul Frommer and I were credited for apprehending (without incident) and executing arrest warrants on Navarro at his place of employment in Coney Island. This guy was an extremely dangerous character, who had earlier fled from Puerto Rico after assaulting two persons with a firearm in Puerto Rico's San Lorenzo section. Warrants were pending for his arrest in that jurisdiction.

In his letter to the NYPD Police Commissioner, Police Chief Beres made numerous comments about our 70th Squad team, including our Commanding Officer, Captain Arthur Deutsch, for our professionalism, efficiency and risk of personal safety in this apprehension."

There was a humorous term called "dickie waver", which described a situation that was anything but funny.

The Midwood Civic Action Council (MCAC), a community group of block associations, reported that a 24-year-old man "regularly disrobes in his front window, begins masturbating while small children walk past his house, and makes all sorts of noises to attract attention to his performance." He'd also allegedly attempted, on numerous occasions, to coax children as young as five and six into his home. This pervert asserted that he was a Black Belt in karate, so local residents feared reprisals, if they were to take any action.

The 70th Detective Squad was assigned by Captain Arthur Deutsch (Commanding Officer of the 70th Precinct) to investigate. The team then consisted of Sergeant William Batista, Detective Joseph Fogarty and me (Detective Rosen). We conducted our investigation in such a way that it was noted that we "showed a sensitivity and concern that made the mothers of the children involved feel comfortable and respected."

Though the MCAC "brought a busload of people to court," the degenerate defendant, named Kagan had already pleaded guilty. He was given a mere Conditional Discharge (ACD), meaning that if he encountered no further violations for six months, his record would be expunged. Many thought this to be a travesty of justice.

However, not long afterwards Kagan was arrested again, this time by Detective Cawley of the 60th Detective Squad. Kagan was charged with exposing himself in front of a 10-year-old girl. This time, he went to jail. Most importantly, the joint efforts of our 70 Squad team in coordination with the 60 Squad enabled us to intervene before he more seriously hurt someone's child.

In early September 1979, I was reassigned to the 60th Detective Squad on Coney Island. For two weeks there had been indiscriminate shootings, with three people wounded and a number of car windows shot out. These shootings occurred at night, and were directed from an above, sniper position in the vicinity of a housing project on Surf Avenue and West 20th Street.

The 60th Detective Squad was headed by Commanding Officer Sgt. James McNiff. Detective George Murphy and I were the ones investigating. While canvassing the area, we enlisted the assistance of residents and housing maintenance men. We checked the roofs for spent shells and alerted neighbors of the danger at hand. Then a phone tip provided the police with a street name: "Papito", which we ran down with our street sources.

On September 11, 1979, we arrested Antonio "Papito" Roman, 18, Miguel Lopez, 17 and a 13-year-old boy, not identified, because of his age. After their arrest, the three were transported to the 60th Precinct Station House for processing. In Roman's 8th floor apartment we found a .22 caliber rifle and 100 rounds of ammunition.

The trio reported that they had shot from the apartment windows, passing the rifle around for each to snipe with. Though they knew that they could hurt someone, they offered no explanation for their actions. Roman and Lopez were charged with Assault. Because Lopez was a juvenile, his case was referred to Family Court, and the boy's charge was Reckless Endangerment.

My life was changed on September 27, 1979 when I became a father, as my wife Christine gave birth to our daughter, Jodi Michelle. Just two months and three days after she came into the world I would again receive a monumental change in my life. When it happened, I considered Jodi Michelle as my "good luck charm".

On November 30, 1979, "Pursuant to a Certificate of the Mayor", the Police Department, City of New York issued Personnel Order No. 400, whereby five other Police Officers and I (still assigned to the 60th Detective Squad) and were designated as DETECTIVE-INVESTIGATOR. Finally, I'd been promoted to Gold Shield status.

This meant that my White Shield (# 13112) was to be "put away", and I would carry the Gold Shield thereafter. When my father retired, he requested that they put a hold on his (gold) shield, anticipating that I would become a detective. So, it was a special honor to receive my Dad's Gold Shield (# 749).

Midwood Civic Action Council, Inc.

1250 EAST 9Th STREET
BROOKLYN, NEW YORK, 11230
(212) 258-2471

March 3, 1979

Police Commissioner Robert McGuire
1 Police Plaza
New York, New York

Dear Sir:

It is my pleasure to write to you in praise of one Arthur Deutsch, Commanding Officer of the 70 Pct.

I do this with great conviction and sincerity. The Midwood Civic Action Council has had dealings with your department since its inception, not all of them of the most pleasant nature. Today, the people of Midwood can rest assured that their precinct is being managed by a fair, conscientious, and affable gentleman. This combination of qualities is particularly important in these times of diminished funds and services.

I would like to give you some concrete examples of the relationship Captain Deutsch has established with our community. One of our block associations (out of 60) came forward with a terrible problem. It seems that a 24 year old man regularly disrobes in his front window, begins masturbating, and makes all sorts of noises to attract attention to his performance. On several occasions he has allegedly tried to coax five and six year olds into his home. Compounding the problem is the assertion that the man in question is a "black-belt" in Karate, and the residents live in fear of reprisal for any actions that they might want to take.

Captain Deutsch spent a great deal of his time finding the best route for us to proceed with this complaint. He sought and received the full cooperation of Det. Sgt. Philip Batista, Det. Foggarty, and Det. Rosen of the 70 Det. Division in this matter. All of these men showed a sensitivity and concern that made the mothers of the children involved feel comfortable and respected.

MCAC brought a busload of people to court to watch the I.M.R.C. in operation. Unfortunately, Mr. Kagan, the accused, had pleaded guilty and been given an ACD before that date. Last night, Mr. Kagan was arrested by

Midwood Civic Action Council, Inc

AC

1250 EAST 9Th STREET
BROOKLYN, NEW YORK, 11230

JAMES P. TENNEY
President

SYLVIA PADOW
Vice-President

ISRAEL KIRSCH
Recording Secretary

RUTH SILVER
Corres. Secretary

SAUL KLEIN
Financial Secretary

LEWIS ALSTER
Treasurer

DOMINICK BARBARINO
Past President and Founder

EXECUTIVE BOARD

ALLAN AUERBACH
ARTHUR BERNER
SHELLY BICKENSTOCK
PETER BONOWITZ
RUBIN BRAUNSTEIN
ALLEN BROD
FAYE BROD
DAVID BURG
BERNARD DANZIG
CAROLYN DOLLY
MARIE ENGLEHARDT
TOBY FRIEDMAN
JERROLD GARSON
SAM GEWERTZMAN
STANLEY GOODMAN
ELLEN GREENBERG
SIDNEY GRUNDLAND
RICHARD HENDLER
SANDER HIRTH
NAT JACOBS
JULIUS KAPLAN
ROBERT KASZIRER
JACK KATZ
S. ASHER KLEIN
BERNARD KUSHEL
SOL LARGA
ROSE LEDERMAN
STANLEY LEFKOWITZ
HAROLD LEVY
ABRAHAM LEWIS
BENJAMIN LIPOWSKY
LILLIAN LAMPERT
ELAINE MATIAS
MARY MOORE
LORETTA MORA
LEON REINISCH
LEO REITMAN
ABRAHAM RIFF
HERB ROMM
SANDY RUBIN
AVNER RUZI
BUNNY SCHNEIDER
ALAN SCHWARTZ
BERNARD SILVER
MATTHEW SIMPSON
MELVIN SINGER
ANNE SMITH
SAM SMITH
JERRY STERN
TOBY TAYLOR
HELEN TENNEY
BONNIE TYLR
LOUISE VINCIGUERRA
DONALD WAHL
BARBARA WATERMAN
BURTON WEINER
MARK ZIPPER
IRWIN ZUCKER

-2-   3-3-79

(212) 258-2471

Det. Cawley of the 61 Pct. on the charge of exposing
himself in front of a 10 year old girl. This marks
a great victory for Midwood since it shows the true
coordination of two precincts, their Commanding Officers
Baumart and Deutsch, the community, and people willing
to step forward and stand up for justice.

Another example of Captain Deutsch's rapport with Midwood involves his quarterly public reports at our
general membership meetings. Here, with 500 citizens
present, the Captain takes on all questioners in a
frank and candid manner.

The Most important link MCAC has to the Police is a
voice in times of emergency. This, of course, is 911's
function (We hope your efforts to increase its efficiency
will be fruitful!). Second only to emergency, is the
need for a constant connection between the Police
and the people. This we have with Captain Deutsch.
Hardly a week passes without a conversation between
the two of us. I let the Captain know of situations
people of the blocks have brought forward (recognizing
that some "facts" are unfounded) and he lets me know
of progress in areas of mutual concern. The members
of MCAC know that he is out there working for them.

All this is not to say that we don't have our differences.
From time to time problems do arise. Our organization
tries to chart a course that gets it involved in all
sorts of entanglements. As a complainer, I feel especially
fortunate to be complaining to an open-minded, honest
administrator. As a citizen of Midwood, I feel that
our opinions do carry weight with Captain Deutsch.

In closing, I would share two thoughts with you. First,
MCAC is glad to have such a fine commanding officer
of the 70 Pct. and we are going to fight to keep the
70 Pct. even with coterminality. Second that we most
cordially invite you to meet our membership at our
March 28, 1979 meeting at Edward R. Murrow High School
so that you might share your thoughts on crime prevention
with us.

Please let me know if it will be possible for you to
attend so that we might adequately plan our agenda

Yours truly,

James P. Tenney, Pres.

P.O. 158-15)

POLICE DEPARTMENT

NEW YORK, N.Y. 10038

Police Officer Gary Rosen
70th P.I.U.

Dear Officer Rosen:

      Congratulations, you have been selected to attend the Tenth Homicide Investigators Course to be conducted by the Detective Bureau.

      The course will bring together a broad spectrum of Judges, District Attorneys, Medical Examiners, police experts and personnel from other outside agencies to instruct homicide investigators. I feel this course is absolutely necessary to acquaint the experienced investigator with the tremendous changes that have occurred in recent years in our criminal justice system. The course's primary objective will be to increase the knowledge of the homicide investigator and thereby enhance his effectiveness.

Location:	New York State Armory, 125 W. 14th St. New York City
Dates:	Monday, April 17, 1978 to Friday, April 28, 1978
Hours:	0900 to 1700 hours
Registration:	0900 hours, Monday, April 17, 1978
Dress:	Business Attire

      Investigators selected to attend will be evaluated on their course note folder, class participation and daily interest.

Sincerely,

James T. Sullivan
CHIEF OF DETECITVES

Misc. 243 (Rev. 2-78)

CIVILIAN COMPLAINT REVIEW BOARD
POLICE DEPARTMENT, CITY OF NEW YORK
200 PARK AVENUE SOUTH   at 17th STREET
NEW YORK, N.Y. 10003   •   TELEPHONE 477-7550

MEMBERS OF THE BOARD
A. BERNARD KELLAND, *Chairperson*
PAMELA D. DELANEY, *Vice Chairperson*

NELSON ALMONTE
MICHAEL AMAROSA
ALLAN J. GRAHAM
WILLIAM E. PERRY

WILLIAM T. JOHNSON
Executive Director
EDWARD C. CIFFONE
Deputy Director

JUN 14 1978

RE: CCRB NO. 815/78

Dear P.O. Rosen:

A complaint received at the Civilian Complaint Review Board in connection with which you were interviewed, has been investigated by our staff and a report prepared. The Board has reviewed that complaint and found that the allegations have not been substantiated. The Police Commissioner has approved that recommendation.

Pursuant to the provisions of Chapter 21, Rules and Procedures, New York City Police Department, the facts of this complaint are confidential and no notation of any kind shall be made in your personal record folder on file with the Department.

Thank you for your cooperation in this matter.

Very truly yours,

William T. Johnson
Executive Director
Civilian Complaint
Review Board

WTJ/jd

P.O. Gary Rosen, #13112
70th Pct.

Ro5éN
FILE

DEPARTMENT OF POLICE SERVICE
P. O. BOX 848 · BELDEN STATION
CITY OF NORWALK. CONNECTICUT · 06852

Address All Communications to
JOSEPH W. BERES, JR.
CHIEF OF POLICE

HONORABLE WILLIAM A. COLLINS
MAYOR

POLICE COMMISSIONERS
——
William J. Lawless, Jr.
RALPH E. IRELAND

November 27, 1978

Mr. Robert J. McQuire
Commissioner
New York City Police Department
#1 Police Plaza
Manhattan, New York

Re: CARMELLO NAVARRO

Dear Commissioner:

On November 7, 1978 Officers in my department developed information
that one, Carmello Navarro, had fled from our jurisdiction to the
Coney Island section of Brooklyn, New York. Carmello Navarro was
being sought by this department as a result of a shot gun murder
and (3)counts of assault with intent to commit murder (2)by shotgun
and (1) by knife.

It is a great personal pleasure to bring to your attention the
efficiency and professionalism in which ·Sgt. William Battista, Det.
Paul Frolier and Det. Gary Rosen displayed in the apprehension and
execution of our arrest warrants at his place of employment in the
Coney Island section of Brooklyn. Carmello Navarro's apprehension
by these officers with officers from my department was accomplished
without incident and thereby removing from our society an extremely
dangerous individual. It is of note that Carmello Navarro fled
from Puerto Rico after similarly assaulting two subjects with a firearm in the San Lorenzo section of Puerto Rico and presently has pending
warrants for his arrest from that jurisdiction.

The spirit of cooperation to accomplish a mutual goal is a deed com-
mendable. I would like to personally thank you and the officers
concerned as well as their Commanding Officer Captain Arthur Deutsch
of the 70th Pct., 154 Lawrence Avenue, Brooklyn, N.Y. for their
professionalism , efficiency and risk of personal safety in this
apprehension.

Commissioner Robert J.McQuire
Re: CARMELLO NAVARRO
November 27, 1978

Page #2

Once again, I personally commend you and the officers of your
department for an outstanding performance.

Sincerely yours,

Joseph W. Beres, Jr.
Chief of Police

JWB:ham
cc: Capt. Arthur Deutsch
    Commanding Officer
    70th Pct. NYC P.D.
    154 Lawrence Avenue
    Brooklyn, NY 11230

    Sgt. Battista
    Det. Frolier
    "   Rosen

Patrolmen's Benevolent Association

Of The City of New York, Incorporated
250 Broadway • New York, N.Y. 10007 • (212) 233-5531

OFFICE OF THE PRESIDENT

July 18, 1979

ROSEN GARY M
6 WINDHAM LOOP
STATEN ISL   NY
10314

Dear Member:

To a great extent, the benefits that the PBA is able to win for the members and their families depend upon the way in which the public views us as police officers. If they think of us as brave, dedicated men and women, our task in Albany and at City Hall is easier.

For that reason, the exceptional performance for which you received a departmental award is important not only to you and to the department, but to every one of your fellow officers now and in the future.

On their behalf and on my own, I am proud to congratulate you on your outstanding achievement.

Fraternally,

Samuel DeMilia
President

Part Four
Gold Shield

Gary Rosen
Promoted to Detective
November 30, 1979

POLICE DEPARTMENT
CITY OF NEW YORK

November 30, 1979.

Personnel Order No. 400

UNIFORM PERSONNEL

1-   DETECTIVE DESIGNATION AWARDED:

7-   Pursuant to a Certificate of the Mayor, the following named
Police Officers are designated as DETECTIVE - INVESTIGATOR:

Effective 1600, November 30, 1979.

		Com'd.
Gary M. Rosen	865622	60 Pct.(I.U.)
Robert H. Carter	860948	73 " "
Michael Clark,Jr.	858330	10 (P.D.U.)
Patrick J. Naughton	854918	32 "
Leonard S. Caruso	854590	34 "
Michael A. Greco	849019	52 "

Chapter Ten

On April 21, 1980, I was transferred to Staten Island, with Crimes Against Persons Detective Squad, based in the Borough Headquarters in the 122nd Precinct. As named, we were assigned with investigating everything deemed a crime against a person: Homicides, Robberies, Assaults, Sex Crimes, Kidnappings, etc.

The Crimes Against Property Squad worked out of the 120th Precinct. They were assigned such cases as Burglaries, Larcenies and Missing Persons.

One of my first cases of note in my new assignment was the overnight homicide of a young man who was believed to have been breaking into cars in early August, 1980. Though not immediately identified, we found the victim on a sidewalk in front of 29 Spring Street, in the Concord section of Staten Island with multiple stab wounds and a tote bag strapped to his left shoulder. In the bag were a wire coat hanger, flashlight and screwdriver – tools known to be used in burglaries. In our search of his clothing, we discovered a small amount of cash in 1 and 5 dollar bills, several coins, a pack of menthol cigarettes and a medallion. As there was no wallet or other form of identifying the body, we checked the missing persons reports and other records (such as fingerprints – provided he had a criminal record) to find out who he was. The victim was a white male who appeared to be in his mid-twenties, about 5' 8" tall, weighing approximately 150 pounds, with straight black hair, brown eyes and a mustache. He was dressed in a black T-shirt, jeans and blue sneakers.

The Squad Supervisor for this case was Sergeant Patrick Bradley. Detective James Mercer was assigned to investigate and I was the assisting Detective. Detective Mercer's father, also a cop, had been killed in the line of duty.

The body was found at about 6:30 on the next morning by Chris Olert, a reporter for the Staten Island Advance, a Staten Island newspaper who was bicycling his way to work. He made contact with police from the nearby Doctor's Hospital. Detectives and patrolmen canvassed the area, interviewing neighbors, some of whom had been awakened between 3 and 3:30 am by a "disturbance". One resident heard "vulgar language during an argument", but no one claimed to have seen the altercation. Persons with information were asked to call a special hotline (987-7935), where all calls would be kept confidential.

After the body was identified as Greg Dente, his father, Louis Dente posted a $10,000.reward for information leading to the arrest and conviction of the killer. Formerly from Staten Island himself, the elder Mr. Dente was an insurance executive with a firm in New Jersey, where he was now residing. He'd offered up this reward because he felt certain that someone had witnessed the argument his son had had, just before he was stabbed to death, and that the fight that led to Greg's death may have been seen by someone in the neighborhood. Detective Mercer and I concurred with Louis Dente's belief that there had been witnesses.

Detective Mercer and I reconstructed the scene from the night of the murder, at times following a trail of blood. The altercation seemed to have begun on Hunter Street, where the victim was likely stabbed once in the back before Dente was able to cross into Spring Street, where he was again stabbed in the back and collapsed. One of the two knife wounds in the back was below his left rib cage, and the other further down, toward the center of his lower back.

We worked this case for well over a month, but were forced to leave it unresolved. Despite the elder Mr. Dente's reward, no one came forward with definitive information. This Concord neighborhood was where a number of NYC cops and firefighters lived. Our investigation uncovered clues which pointed to a suspect who was living up the hill from where the attack originated. We'd surmised that a man had caught Greg Dente breaking into cars parked in front of his house on the street where this man lived, and confronted Dente. Unfortunately, we were unable to amass sufficient evidence for an arrest.

Early on the morning of June 19, 1980, Patrick Myers, 23, of 27 Warren St., Stapleton was shot on a Stapleton street corner. He was struck by three bullets: once in the left chest, once in the left shoulder, and once in the right arm. The shooting occurred at 1:30 am on Young and Targee Streets. Myers managed to stagger four blocks, collapsing on the sidewalk in front of his home. He was found, lying in a pool of blood by Felicia Thomas, a friend. Mr. Myers was rushed to the U.S. Public Health Service Hospital, Clifton, where doctors worked on him for several hours before he was stabilized sufficiently to be taken into surgery for the removal of the bullets.

Just days before, on June 15, Glen Jones, 22, of 741 Van Duzer St. was shot, a mere block from the Myers shooting. Both victims were reportedly friends, but we could not establish a link between the two incidents. Jones had not been seriously injured in Sunday's shooting.

A traffic accident in Clifton happened an hour before Myers was shot involving Harold Brown, 50, of 220 Osgood Ave., Stapleton and Patrick Francis, 21, of 824 Lafayette Ave., New Brighton. At the site of the accident, opposite 185 Parkhill Ave., Brown reportedly argued with Francis and several passengers in Francis' car, after Brown was unable to produce his driver's license and registration. Brown then allegedly threatened to go home and get a gun.

About an hour later the police received simultaneous calls that a man was shot and that another man was roaming the Stapleton area with a gun. Several units responded to these calls.

Brown was arrested in front of the Zebra Lounge at 595 Targee St., Concord. When Police Officers of the 120, John Garza and Frank Salt approached Brown, he handed them a brown canvas bag, telling them that his gun was in the bag. The .38 caliber revolver they found was fully loaded.

Initially, we believed that Brown may have shot Myers, but the timeline didn't work. Brown had been too far away from the shooting when he was picked up by police. Our full scale investigation began, as we reached out to street informants for information that may lead to the assailant.

However, Brown was taken to the St. George Precinct, where he was identified by several people involved in the auto accident. They reported that Brown had threatened them with a gun. He was held on a weapons charge and accused of menacing Francis and the occupants of his car.

On June 24, 1980 I arrested Bernard Johnson, 26 at 9:30 pm at his residence at 156 Drumgoole Rd. East. He had a cache of fireworks in his home, mainly giant sparklers and different kinds of aerial rockets. But it was for his sale of far more dangerous fireworks, reported by witnesses, to several youths from an ice cream truck the night before that I caught the case.

Johnson had been selling explosives from the truck, ranging in power from mats of firecrackers to cherry bombs, ash cans and M80s. A 14 year old kid purchased one of these M80s, equivalent to a quarter stick of dynamite. When he set it off, it blew up in his left hand, causing severe injury. From the Mr. Softee-type ice cream truck, we confiscated $2,500 in fireworks. The Brooklyn South-Staten Island Public Morals Squad was notified, and became involved with the Crimes Against Persons Squad on the case.

Though we issued only one summons to one of the youths who bought the explosives from his truck, we also arrested two men suspected of supplying Johnson with the fireworks. Hidden in the roof of a two-car garage at 20 Morningstar Rd. in Elm Park we discovered $75,000 worth of fireworks. The men were loading a van with cartons of fireworks, at the time of the arrest. Records found on the premises referred to Johnson as "Buddy the Ice Cream Man." Johnson was unarmed at the time of the arrest and offered no resistance.

In November, 1980 a Sears employee got into his white 1972 Cadillac. When he put the car into Drive and started forward, a pipe bomb rigged to the car's gas tank exploded, indicating that the device was attached to the car's transmission.

Murray Seidler, 46, a manager at the Sears department store in the New Springville Mall, was fortunately uninjured in the explosion. Arriving at work that morning, Seidler had parked his Caddy opposite the entrance to the Verrazano Restaurant, on the Marsh Ave. side of the mall's lot. It was there the entire day, so we began canvassing the mall for witnesses who may have seen someone working on the parked car.

Two factors contributed to Seidler's survival. Of course the Cadillac was a heavy, sturdy car, according the driver some degree of protection. Most critical, though, is that the car's gas tank was almost entirely full, leaving very little vapor to catch fire. Had the tank been closer to empty, the propane tanks affixed to the car's undercarriage would've ignited the vapors and exploded the gas tank.

At 2pm on November 16, 1980 I arrested Julio Quinones, 30 for sexual abuse and endangering the welfare of several children. Mr. Quinones was employed as a counselor for the *Mission of the Immaculate Virgin*, Mount Loretto – an orphanage. He'd been working for 6 months with the Life Skills Unit, a cottage that houses 14 year old boys.

Quinones was accused of inviting the youngsters to his apartment at 174 Grandview Ave., Mariners Harbor the evening before. There, he allegedly supplied them with marijuana, amphetamine and vodka and orange juice drinks, before fondling a 13 year old girl and then watching her and a 14 year old boy engage in sexual intercourse.

At 7 o'clock the following morning, Quinones reportedly refused to allow the girl to return to her mother's home in the Bronx. The girl ran to a store on Richmond Terrace, where she asked the store owner to notify police.

Individual interviews with the youngsters involved were consistent. We then spoke with the facility's security force, who detained Quinones until I, along with other members of the Crimes Against Persons Squad arrived to arrest him.

During this time Lieutenant Ellen King had been setting up a Sex Crimes Unit and found that some police officers who investigated such crimes were unsympathetic. The clothing style of the time included miniskirts and halter tops for women. In some circles, it was believed that scantily clad women were exhibiting suggestive behavior (whether professional prostitutes, or girls simply out for the night), and might somehow be "inviting" sexual assault. In fact many of the women raped or sexually assaulted had never reported the rape at the time of the crime.

Lieutenant King was putting together a Sex Crimes seminar to take place at the 14th St. Armory in Manhattan, the first of its kind. Several hundred detectives who worked in various agencies throughout the Northeast were invited to attend. As I was one of the youngest detectives working some of these crimes, Lieutenant King thought that I might be better able than older detectives to relate to the young victims. So, she asked me if I'd be willing to speak about the effect that such incidents had, both on victims and responding police officers.

In an effort to have the officers better understand the plight of young women who'd been raped, the question of the victims' reluctance to come forward to report the crime came up. I created a hypothetical scenario, asking the audience, "If you were in Central Park at night, were attacked and sexually molested or sodomized, how many of you would report the crime?" No one raised a hand. I explained that the stigma of admitting to having been victimized, coupled with the trauma of the attack, made reporting these crimes difficult. The victims almost always felt ostracized. I emphasized the need to be less hasty and more sensitive and compassionate in responding to such cases.

Soon after the seminar I received – on official City of New York Police Department letterhead – a personal letter, dated December 3, 1980 from the Chief of Detectives, James T. Sullivan. In the letter he wrote that, "I wish to express my sincere appreciation for your excellent contribution to the Sex Crimes Investigation Seminar." He closed with "Many thanks for your demonstration of expertise in interviewing techniques."

At that time there was a Sex Crimes Unit, which some years later became known as the Special Victims Unit (SVU).

Weeks later (December 20, 1980 I was also selected as the alternate D.E.A. (Detectives' Endowment Association, the union that represented detectives) delegate by Thomas J. Scotto, DEA Trustee, Staten Island Area.

DETECTIVE-INVESTIGATORS

Effective 0800, April 21, 1980. (See NOTE page 7)

From Commands indicated to Commands specified:

		From Com'd.	To Com'd.
Gary M. Rosen	865622	60 Pct.(I.U.)	P.B.S.I., Cri.vs.Pers.Sqd
Tony E. Flynn	865058	81 Pct.(I.U.)	"
Antonio Rodriguez	857262	Bklyn Det.Area, Robb.-Burg.Sqd.	P.B.S.I., Cri.vs.Prop.Sqd
Kevin J. Egan	855237	Narc.Div.(O.C C.B.)	Bklyn Det.Area
George F. Reilly	860755	"	"

POLICE DEPARTMENT
NEW YORK, N.Y. 10038

P.D. 158-151

December 3, 1980

Detective Gary Rosen
Crimes Against Persons Squad
122 Precinct
2320 Hylan Boulevard
New Dorp, Staten Island 10306

Dear Detective Rosen,

      I wish to express my sincere appreciation for your excellent contribution to the Sex Crimes Investigation Seminar.

      Response to the training program has been outstanding and I attribute this to exemplary faculty and student participation.

      Many thanks for your demonstration of expertise in interviewing techniques.

Yours truly,

James T. Sullivan
CHIEF OF DETECTIVES

DETECTIVES' ENDOWMENT ASSOCIATION
POLICE DEPARTMENT CITY OF NEW YORK, INC.

299 Broadway, Suite 516, New York, New York 10007 • 349-0360

December 20, 1980

To: Commanding Officer, Crimes Against Persons Squad.

Please be advised that as of this date, Det Gary Rosen, assigned to your command has been selected as the alternate DEA delegate.

If for any reason the assigned delegate can not attend the monthly meeting, Det Rosen will then be entitled to the same excusal as per M.E.O. #75.

Thomas J Scotto
DEA Trustee
Staten Island Area

277

123

Gary Rosen and Daughter Jodi Michelle
Staten Island Crimes Against Persons Squad Room
1984

Gary
and
Christine

Chapter Eleven

On December 3, 1980, an Emerson Hill woman who was viciously assaulted on the street, suffering from a fractured skull and was admitted to Staten Island Hospital in critical condition. While not directly assigned to the case, I joined every detective in the Crimes Against Persons Squad in working to solve the mystery of this heinous attack.

A neighbor had found the woman, Sophia Enzinger, 41, of 14 Wilson View Place lying in a pool of blood in the roadway near 7 Douglas Road. The woman who'd discovered her put Mrs. Enzinger in her car and drove her home, before she realized the severity of the injury and called for an ambulance.

The victim was able to recall her return trip home from work on the X-14 express bus from Manhattan, when she exited the bus at Richmond Road and began walking up Douglas Road. Shortly before 6 pm, someone struck her on the right side of her forehead with a heavy object. As reported by the victim's husband, her purse, jewelry and cash were intact, indicating no known motive for the attack. Our initial search for evidence was made extremely difficult, as Douglas Road was dark and there was a cold wind blowing, with several inches of leaves on the ground. We sought the assistance of the Transit Authority, to provide the names of all the bus drivers who used the Richmond Rd. route on the night of the assault, and also asked for the public's cooperation. Again, a confidential report line was set up for the public to telephone any information to 987-7935.

As the investigation was being conducted, Mrs. Enzinger underwent surgery for the injuries to her head for over an hour.

On the very same day, three hours later, a second woman was assaulted after getting off a number 107 bus from Manhattan on her way home. However, we weren't informed of this second attack until the following day, as the injuries she'd sustained were not considered serious at the time, and we were still canvassing the Emerson Hill area of the earlier attack. After she was bludgeoned, Carol Corson, 48, of 4 Parsons Place in the West Brighton section was reportedly taken by her husband to St. Vincent's Medical Center, where she was treated for her injuries (receiving several stitches) and released from the hospital.

Mrs. Corson had been struck from behind, around 9 pm after exiting the bus, as she walked along City Blvd. and Huron Place. She was a mere 40 feet from her home before her assailant pounced. Both of the assaulted women were struck by a blunt object. This second attack differed from the earlier one on Mrs. Enzinger in that Mrs. Corson's tan leather shoulder bag and a blue shopping bag were ripped from her arms and taken. The purse had contained a mere $3. The shopping bag was later recovered.

One of Mrs. Corson's neighbors reported hearing her scream, raced to her aid and alerted Mr. Corson, who rushed her to the hospital. After being released from St. Vincent's, she experienced dizzy spells later in the day and returned to the hospital, presenting with signs of a concussion. Doctors determined that Mrs. Corson was bleeding internally as a result of the assault, and she was placed in St. Vincent's intensive care unit, listed in guarded condition.

That same night Mrs. Enzinger, following her surgery the day before at Staten Island Hospital, was listed in satisfactory condition.

There had been no known record of Staten Island muggings where this method of knocking a victim down was employed, so we cautiously confirmed the possibility that the two attacks were related. The Emerson Hill and West Brighton sections of Staten Island were a significant distance from each other, but close enough for the same assailant to have been at the scene of both attacks.

Some evidence indicated that the blunt object used in the assaults may have been a pipe.

A man was reportedly seen in the area, running down Douglas Road shortly after Mrs. Enzinger was struck, but no solid evidence linked any man to either of the incidents. Unfortunately, there were no arrests made on these two violent crimes. These cases became known as those of "The Staten Island Basher."

In early January, 1981 Detective Cathy Bertolino and I were investigating a stabbing at a motel in the Grasmere section of Staten Island, when we discovered additional crimes at the same location.

Late Saturday night there had been a stabbing reported at the Staten Island Motor Lodge at 481 Hylan Boulevard. William Bergsma, 28, a resident at the motel had been stabbed in the stomach as a result of an altercation with two other men. After questioning Bergsma at the hospital, Detective Bertolino and I went to the motel to interview other residents. When we got there we found cameras and other equipment being removed from his room and placed in a car. We then questioned a number of people at the motel, and released all but one.

The other person, William Prince, 18, who told us that he lived there, was arrested, accused of Robbery and Possession of a Weapon. We found evidence in the room that Prince shared with Bergsma that linked them to the armed robbery of two women in the parking lot of the Staten Island Mall, New Springville on December 23, 1980. Among the items we found was a .38 caliber revolver.

The car parked in front of their room, which reportedly was used by the men, had been stolen from Brooklyn. In fact, we uncovered a robbery ring that took in a number of New York City's boroughs. We learned the identities of two Midland Beach brothers who were implicated in the stabbing. They were Thomas McConnell, 23, and his 20-year old brother, Christopher, both of 118 Kiswick Street. The two were arrested, accused of Robbery, First Degree and Criminal Possession of a Weapon.

Piecing together what we'd discovered, we believed that at least six persons, apparently in an attempt to avoid detection, worked in interchanging teams which were committing armed robberies. Most of these were street robberies in Staten Island and other boroughs. We also had reason to believe that this ring was involved with stolen cars, as well as illicit drug-related activities. The two rooms they rented at the Staten Island Motor Lodge were being used as a base for their gang operations. Related arrests were later made by police in other boroughs.

I was assigned to investigate an incident which occurred on April 2, 1981. At 1:30 pm James Steinhilber, 24, of Brighton Beach stopped his beer delivery truck at the corner of North Burger Ave. and Wayne Street to deliver beer to a grocery store.

Two teenagers confronted Steinhilber, forcibly taking his cash and checks. They also took six cases of beer.

Another case I was assigned to investigate began with an Assault and Robbery of a woman who lived in the New Springville section of Staten Island. This victim, a young lady, was the daughter of my father's friend, Patrolman Heshy Dembin. She worked as a nurse at St. Vincent's Hospital in Staten Island, and the incident took place close to the hospital.

On April 14, 1981, shortly after 3 pm Jane Dembin, 23, returned from a bank visit to her car, which was parked at the intersection of Castleton Avenue and Taylor Street. At first, she didn't notice that there was a man in her car, as she began to drive away. Ms. Dembin told me that everything had happened so fast, that she couldn't offer a better description of the skell, described to be in his 20's, 6 feet tall, about 175 pounds. He'd grabbed her by the throat, while wielding a hammer in his other hand, demanding her money. Ms Dembin gave the assailant $300 from her purse, then slammed on her car's brakes and jumped out of the car. The suspect followed, catching up to her, and ripping two gold chains from her neck, before fleeing toward Richmond Terrace.

There had recently been a series of gold chain snatchings, as well as muggings in the area. It was believed that the same people were doing the robberies, but this was the first time that someone had actually gotten into a victim's car. I took a personal interest in this case and canvassed the area of the occurrence thoroughly, but was unfortunately unable to find any witnesses to the robbery.

Less than two weeks later, on April 26th as we continued our investigation, Dominick Ferraro, 30 years old, of 322 Clove Road, West Brighton was arrested on the Verrazano-Narrows Bridge, following a car chase from Midland Beach. Ferraro had allegedly robbed a woman who was selling hot dogs from a stand outside Egbert Junior High School in Midland Beach. The robbery netted the suspect only $15, but he'd allegedly threatened her with a fake weapon, demanding the keys to her car. When the woman refused to hand over her keys, Ferraro ran up Midland Avenue to Hylan Blvd.

As he got to Hylan Blvd. he ran up to a woman putting air in the tires of her car at the Mobil service station at the corner. As this woman, Hermana Mondido was putting air in the tire, Ferraro jumped into the driver's seat and raced away. In the car with Ferraro were Mrs. Mondido's daughter, Marilyn Mondido and granddaughter, Jennifer Mondido, 18 months old.

After driving himself and his two involuntary passengers several blocks down Hylan Blvd., Ferraro allegedly stopped the car, pointed the fake gun at Ms. Mondido and demanded her purse. Instead of complying, she opened the car door and fled with the baby in her arms.

By this time the police had rushed to the service station, had interviewed Mrs. Mondido and broadcast an alarm for the vehicle. A patrol car from the 120th Precinct spotted the car with Ferraro at the wheel, heading for the bridge, and initiated a chase. A second patrol car from the 120th joined the chase, and the two police cars brought the suspect to a halt on the Verrazano-Narrows Bridge.

Ferraro was taken to the 122nd Precinct stationhouse in New Dorp, where he was identified by the Mondidos. Not much later, the owner of the hot dog stand was brought to Central Booking at the 120th Precinct stationhouse, St. George, where she identified Ferraro as the man who'd robbed her. A man fitting his description was also reported to have held up a service station on Cary Ave., West Brighton, where he brandished what appeared to be a small pistol, escaping with approximately $250.

Following Ferraro's arrest, there was a markedly diminished number of robberies in Staten Island.

STATEN ISLAND SAVINGS BANK
STAPLETON, STATEN ISLAND
NEW YORK 10304

JOHN L. F. SIPP
CHAIRMAN OF THE BOARD
AND
CHIEF EXECUTIVE OFFICER

April 22, 1981

Detective Gary Rosen
Crimes Against Persons Squad
122nd Precinct
2320 Hylan Boulevard
Staten Island, New York 10306

Dear Detective Rosen:

You and your men conducted yourselves in the most
professional manner on the night our messenger was
held up.

The immediate discovery of the culprits' vehicle
and the return of the courier's pouch with almost
its entire contents within hours after the incident
was indeed reassuring and certainly confirms our
confidence in the Police Department and its various
divisions.

Please accept our grateful appreciation and thanks
for a job well done.

Sincerely,

John L. F. Sipp

JLFS:gh

Staten Island Advance

Copyright © 1981 by Advance Publications Inc.

Staten Island, N.Y. Friday, February 20, 1981

Great Kills man held in murder of friend

Police charged a Great Kills man with the murder of his friend last night after a shotgun discharged in the bedroom of the suspect's home, detectives said.

Douglas Heydt, 19, of 6 Crescent Beach died at approximately 9:30 p.m. in Richmond Memorial Hospital from shotgun wounds in the neck, police said.

According to Staten Island detectives, Heydt apparently was visiting Philip Calvo, 19, of 59 Goodall St. at 5:20 p.m. last night when the incident occurred.

The two men were in a second-floor bedroom of the one-family home while members of the Calvo family were downstairs, according to Sgt. Patrick Bradley of the Crimes Against Persons squad.

"We know there was a struggle for the shotgun," Bradley said. "During the struggle the gun discharged hitting Heydt once in the head."

The gun was loaded with ammunition used for hunting birds, police said. The full blow of the discharge struck Heydt in the right side of the neck, according to police.

Heydt was rushed to Richmond Memorial Hospital shortly after the shooting, police said.

Police said that through an investigation conducted by Detectives Gary Rosen and Catherine Bertolino it was learned that the incident involved a struggle. Calvo was brought to the 122nd Precinct Stationhouse in New Dorp where he was questioned again by detectives after Heydt died, police said.

Calvo, acting on advice from his attorney, refused to speak to police. "We had a situation where we have a man dead, an unregistered gun and the person who was alone with him at the time," Bradley said. At 11 p.m. detectives formally charged Calvo with murder in the second degree.

Police said Calvo, who was at one time employed as a runner for a Manhattan brokerage firm, will be arraigned today in Stapleton Criminal Court.

Heydt worked as a station attendant at a Mobil service station at

Philip Calvo, left, is escorted into the 120th Precinct stationhouse, St. George, by Detective Gary Rosen after Calvo was accused of murdering Douglas Heydt.
S.I. Advance Photo by Tony Carannante

Hylan Blvd. and Nelson Ave., Great Kills. The victim and the suspect were friends for at least five years, police said.

— PAMELA O'SHAUGHNESSY

134

Chapter Twelve

My next case, again worked with Detective Catherine Bertolino, was a murder investigation. Our investigation led to the arrest of a Great Kills man for the shotgun killing of a friend of his in the bedroom of the suspect's home.

Douglas Heydt, 19, of Crescent Beach had apparently come to visit Philip Calvo, 19, of 59 Goodall St. on the evening of the incident. While members of the Calvo family were downstairs in the single family house, the "friends" were in an upstairs bedroom. Following a struggle over a shotgun between Calvo and Heydt, the gun was discharged, hitting Heydt once in the head, with the full force of the blast striking Heydt in the right side of the neck. The gun was loaded with birdshot ammunition.

Heydt was rushed to Richmond Memorial Hospital, where he died at approximately 9:30pm. The gun he was shot with was unregistered, and Calvo was alone with him at the time of the shooting. Calvo was charged with Murder in the Second Degree.

Heydt had worked as a station attendant at a Mobil station at Hylan Blvd. and Nelson Ave., Great Kills. Calvo had at one time been employed as a runner for a Manhattan brokerage firm. The two had reportedly been friends for more than five years.

On March 27, 1981, I was assigned to investigate the robbery of a bank messenger. Louis Vogel, 56, of Port Richmond Center, a retired Housing Authority police officer, was completing his daily rounds for *Staten Island Savings Bank* when the car he was driving was struck by a gray Toyota at Tompkins Ave. and Fingerboard Road.

The driver of the Toyota, in an effort to have Vogel stop, pretended to have hit Vogel's car by accident, though the collision was definitely intentional. As Vogel, who'd pulled to the curb, was attempting to retrieve the insurance card from his glove compartment, he turned his back on the three men who exited the Toyota. These men attacked Vogel, punching him repeatedly. They robbed him of a sack containing checks and savings bonds, as well as his hand gun.

The sack was later recovered in the Toyota, abandoned on Seaver Ave. and Zoe Street in Dongan Hills. Of greater concern was the missing gun. The trio of assailants seemed to have been unarmed at the time of the robbery. Now some very unstable characters had someone else's weapon. Again, the police provided the phone number for anyone who had information to call, offering confidentiality.

In early May of 1981, I worked an investigation of the robbery of a Waldbaum's supermarket at 778 Manor Road in Castleton Corners.

Three men were reported to have entered the store around 7:25 pm, forcing the manager, George Ketcham into an office. After the bandits took an undetermined amount of cash, they fled from the store into a blue car, where the fourth man, a getaway driver, whisked them away.

This became another case of too little information provided, so I asked for community assistance, hoping for details of the robbery or the car's license plate number. Again, we listed a phone number where conversations would be kept strictly confidential.

There were many occasions when I'd be working two or more cases simultaneously. On Friday night, May 1, 1981 at about 5 pm, a police harbor launch fished a body out of the water. The badly decomposed man was discovered floating in the *Kill Van Kull* off the Staten Island side of the Bayonne Bridge near the Elm Park community.

Although we found a wallet in his clothing, we couldn't confirm the identity of the victim, as the decomposition of his corpse indicated that he'd been in the water for a month or more. In fact, we weren't certain if the man had been killed or committed suicide. He appeared to be approximately 20 years old, but age, ID and cause of death determination would await the report from the medical examiner. His body showed no signs of injury or struggle.

Several days later, thanks to dental records, the decomposed body was identified as Ronald Vandermeyde, 19, of 132 Lockman Ave., Mariners Harbor. He'd lived there most of his life, but had been born in Queens. Mr. Vandermeyde was a graduate of the 1980 class at Port Richmond High School, where he'd led the school's bowling team to the finals. He'd also been a member of the West Shore Little League and the Sea Cadets.

This much was known of Mr. Vandermeyde's disappearance: He'd been missing since March 25th, the day before he was to have entered the U.S. Navy as a serviceman.

The young man had reportedly totaled his parent's automobile in an accident on that evening. After he reportedly crashed the car in Graniteville, Ronald had walked away from the accident to make a phone call to home. The young man's parents, Mr. and Mrs. Carl Vandermeyde had reported that their son may have been afraid to come home after wrecking the family car, and he may have also been concerned about being late to report to the Navy the next day.

My investigation led to a scenario where Vandermeyde, accompanied by a group of other young men had gone to the Verrazano Bridge by design, to hang out and to drink beer. Perhaps this had been an impromptu going away social event, as Ronald's send-off to "join the Navy and see the world." The young men had apparently climbed up to the catwalk under the girders of the bridge, where they'd be afforded privacy.

I went to the Triboro Bridge & Tunnel Authority, who cooperated by sending two of their men to accompany me to the Verrazano Bridge. Once there, we climbed up from the roadway to a catwalk that was no more than a grating for a floor, supported by two supporting steel bars beneath. It was there that broken beer bottles were found. As I followed the Authority workers out onto the grated catwalk to the water far below. I'd not walked a few feet when – for the first time in my life – I experienced a fear of heights. The Verrazano had been built extremely high to enable warships to safely pass underneath.

All indications were that Ronald Vandermeyde had accidentally fallen from the bridge, with no signs of foul play. In addition to his parents, he was survived by his paternal grandmother, Tra DeHaas of the Netherlands. The family arranged for cremation and a funeral.

On May 19th, 1981, two decomposed bodies of an unidentified man and woman were discovered in a garbage-strewn wooded area near Claypit Ponds State Park Preserve in Rossville. The bodies were found – wrapped in carpet bundles – by two Con Edison employees at about 3:15pm on Clay Pit Road when they stopped to look at discarded car parts. The area was an illegal dumping ground about a tenth of a mile from Arthur Kill Rd.

The victims, possibly in their 30's, appeared to have been dead 3-4 weeks. Their hands and feet had been bound with inexpensive twine, in apparent gangland fashion. The woman was approximately 5 feet 4 inches tall and heavy-set. The man was at least 6 feet tall, with brown hair. Both were dressed in blue jeans. The woman was wearing a hooded sweatshirt – the man, a Western shirt. On their feet, the woman wore sneakers, while the man was wearing loafers.

Detective Vincent Albanese and I were in charge of the investigation. The two bodies were separately wrapped in rust tweed carpeting of poor quality, at least 10 years old. Each bundle, serving as the pair's initial coffins, were fastened with clothesline from the outside. Inside, we noted blood stains on the carpets which did not indicate heavy bleeding. From this we'd determined that the victims had been killed elsewhere, then the carpet had been cut from a larger swath (perhaps once wall-to-wall) to fit each individually, making transport of the bodies easier.

No identification was found on either body, as were no wallets. However, the woman was wearing a gold chain with a gold "M" charm, along with a gold ring. This suggested that robbery hadn't been a motive. Still, these weren't two male bodies, so we had doubts that this had been an organized crime hit. In fact, we weren't even certain that they were from Staten Island, as Missing Persons in S.I. hadn't yet come up with anything. As I'd told the reporter from the Staten Island Advance, "We are waiting for the medical examiner to determine the cause of death. Once we find that out, we can start working on the identification." The victims were taken to Bellevue Morgue in Manhattan, where an autopsy was expected to be completed within a day.

The next day we learned more from the medical examiner's preliminary autopsy report: the victims both appeared to have been strangled, but strangulation was confirmed solely for the woman's death. It was noted that the man had no puncture wounds on his body.

Though we still had no identification for the two, we were working on a lead that potentially linked the pair to a couple reported missing in Queens on April 10th. A relative of the missing woman from Queens identified the jewelry, via telephone from her upstate New York home. She was expected to travel to Staten Island within the day to view the property, and to bring dental records from the dentist that may have treated the victim. The Queens couple reported missing were a 22 year old woman and a man of 51 years, who had reportedly been dating.

Within a week we were able to identify the two murder victims. Martha Ossite, a bookkeeper from Forest Hills, was actually 21 at the time of her death. Roberto Ramella, 51, of Sunnyside, Queens was an unemployed chef. At this point we concluded that the couple was not killed on Staten Island, but we had not yet determined where the murders had occurred. Having identified them, we needed to trace their backgrounds, determine place of death, and motive.

I had a friend who worked in the carpet industry who noted a cut in the piece of rug that the bodies had been wrapped in. He identified it as a hole to fit the carpet around a radiator. When checking with the Building Department's records, I discovered a common apartment layout that clearly indicated the positioning of a radiator which coincided with the carpet's cut.

We knew that Staten Island was a "dumping place" for bodies, and we were relatively certain that these bodies were mob hits, but

we didn't have enough evidence for an arrest. As with a number
of our cases in Staten Island, some victims were unable to identify
assailants, even after being given the opportunity to view mug
shot photos. In such unresolved instances, we closed these cases,
pending further development.

Shortly after 9 o'clock on the evening of July 30, 1981,
someone rang the doorbell repeatedly at the home of 86 year
old Frank Markey and his wife on Todt Hill Road. Mr. Markey
eventually answered the door, as a gunman forced his way in
the house. The intruder, who was believed to be in his mid-30's,
then forced Mr. Markey into an upstairs bedroom, where he
tied Markey and his 83 year-old wife, Frances, with an extension
cord. The man then ransacked the house, even taking a diamond
engagement ring from Mrs. Markey's finger. Soon after I was
assigned to the case I discovered that a dark-colored Camaro or
Firebird had been parked in front of the house on Todt Hill Rd.,
from about 9:10 - 9:40pm.

At some point Mr. Markey was able to free himself from his
restraints. He hit an alarm button which summoned the police
to the house. Markey and his wife were taken to Staten Island
Hospital, where they were treated for injuries they sustained during
the home invasion. Markey was admitted to the hospital, listed in
satisfactory condition. His wife was treated and released.

Mr. Markey, a wealthy importer of coffee into the U.S.
had what some other private citizens and certain business had: a
direct line to the local police precinct, via a panic button. Markey
may have been set up for the robbery, so we looked into possible
suspects as an "inside job" angle.

Mysterious deaths had struck the South Beach
Psychiatric Center.

The third such death, during the past 3 years under similar
circumstances, was that of a 17 year old mental patient from Bay
Terrace named Andrew Zamora on August 17, 1981. His parents
reported that he'd been admitted to the hospital only 2 nights
earlier, following a midnight attack of paranoia. The South Beach

Psychiatric Center, with 300 beds, was a relatively small state-run facility.

After the boy's mother, Georgette Zamora asked the Staten Island District Attorney to investigate, I was assigned to the case. Mrs. Zamora, sobbingly expressing her disappointment with the hospital's lack of candor, said: "They scared him to death. He was polite and gentle. He listened to everybody." Physically healthy when admitted, the cause of the youth's death was not immediately known, pending an autopsy by the city Medical Examiner.

Although he'd been given drugs before being placed in restraints, two attending physicians speculated that "natural causes" were to blame for his death, according to the Deputy Director of Treatment Services at the center, Linda Breslin. Only one of the two physicians referred to was identified: Dr. Jonathan Kane, a staff psychiatrist. The other was an unnamed doctor, who was said to be affiliated with nearby Staten Island Hospital. Ms. Breslin contended that Zamora died at 5 pm of cardiac arrest, while claiming that a therapy aide had checked the patient 15 minutes before, recording that his vital signs (including pulse and temperature) had been normal.

"This is a very puzzling case," said Ms. Breslin.

While Zamora died in the South Richmond Service Unit, the two previous deaths of young patients, also under restraint, occurred in the hospital's Intensive Care Unit. The two units were the hospital's only locked wards, designed to treat agitated patients.

I noted that Zamora bore no external signs of injury, such as cuts or bruises. However, most of my questions of the South Beach officials went unanswered. They refused to disclose the type of medication Zamora had received, or the length of time he was restrained in a "bed net", citing patient confidentiality. Though Ms. Breslin confirmed that the boy had not attempted suicide, she said that the restraint was applied because Zamora had shown "self-destructive behavior."

The family of the deceased had many questions that remained unanswered by the facility. Mrs. Zamora reported that she'd warned the hospital staff "time and time again" that her son reacted adversely to certain drugs. Following her son's death, she asked what type of medication he'd been given. The response she says she received from Dr. Kane is that he'd have "to look it up."

In fact, the parents said they'd only learned of their son's death during a visit to South Beach at the request of the police, who'd telephoned their home. Mrs. Zamora stated that the hospital staff did not mention the bed net restraint. She said that her husband Gregory was allowed to glance through an open door to identify the body.

"What are they trying to cover up?," she asked. "I won't rest until I find out what's happening."

According to the family, Mr. Gregory Zamora had been turned away from the hospital twice when he'd tried to visit his son at 11 am on Saturday, and again on Monday, the day the boy died.

Georgette Zamora said, "We thought Andrew would be coming home the next day."

Andrew Zamora had reportedly recently returned from a trip to Florida, "nervous and overtired".He was accompanied by his parents when he went to South Beach before dawn on Saturday, and was admitted there with a diagnosis of paranoia. While in Florida Andrew had been interviewed at a private psychiatric facility, the Desisto School in Holly Hill, Florida. His mother said he had expected to start therapy there on September 1st.

"We read about the school in Time magazine. It was supposed to be an excellent place, and Andrew was very excited," she stated.

South Beach's Deputy Director, Ms. Breslin said that the hospital was conducting an internal review of Zamora's death. The State Office of Mental health and the State Commission on Quality of Care for the Mentally Disabled were to be notified. The State officials were to consider the significance of the "clustering" of the three deaths under restraint.

During my investigation I learned that Andrew's father, Gregory, had been repeatedly making threats on personnel at the facility. They'd told me that they indeed feared for their lives. Most importantly, it was revealed that all three deaths were the result of overdoses of Thorazine. This was a frequently used medication at that time, especially at Crisis Stabilization Units. It was intended to calm patients who had been acting out, and required doctors' orders. Because of many similarly noted incidents over the years, Thorazine began to be phased out of practice.

My work with the facility's staff was later noted in a letter from James J. Mahoney, Director, Facility Administration Services at South Beach Psychiatric Center to New York City Police Commissioner, Robert McGuire. In the letter Mr. Mahoney notes that "an individual from the community had been harassing our staff members over the past several months. In response to our complaints, police from the 122 Precinct Crimes Against Persons Unit have met with our staff and have been very helpful in explaining police procedures…we feel that both Sgt. Bradley and Det. Rosen should be commended for their efforts." It was we, from the Crimes Against Persons Squad, that were the detectives responsible for this investigation.

SOUTH BEACH PSYCHIATRIC CENTER

777 Seaview Avenue
Staten Island, New York, 1C305
Telephone (212) 667-2300

LUCY REA SARKIS. M.D
DIRECTOR

LINDA BRESLIN, C.S.W.
DEPUTY DIRECTOR
TREATMENT SERVICES

JAMES J. MAHONEY, M.B A.
DEPUTY DIRECTOR
ADMINISTRATION

KAY WALTERS, M.S., R N.
DEPUTY DIRECTOR
QUALITY ASSURANCE

Det. Gary McRosen
Tax # 865622

January 13th, 1983

Robert Mc Guire
Commissioner of Police
of the City of New York
1 Police Plaza
New York, New York

□ PRECINCT/COMMAND BULLETIN BOARD

□ PRECINCT/COMMAND PERSONNEL FOLDER

[Note: Original Documents Have Been Filed in Personnel Folder at Performance Evaluation Section]

Dear Com. Mc Guire:

    South Beach Psychiatric Center is a New York State Office of Mental Health facility servicing the mental health needs of the western Brooklyn and Staten Island areas. As a public agency, our employees interface with members of the community constantly. From time to time, our employees have been harrassed by community members to the extend that police intervention was necessary.

    As an example of this, an indivdiual from the community had been harrassing our staff members over the past several months. In response to our complaints, police from the 122 Precinct, Crimes Against Persons Unit have met with our staff and have been very helpful in explaining police procedures. In particular, Sgt. Patrick Bradley and Det. Gary Rosen have been immensely cooperative with the administration of South Beach Psychiatric Center in advising employees of the ways of handling any future harrassing incidents. The staff of South Beach Psychiatric Center appreciate the helpful attitude demonstrated by these officers.

    We feel that both Sgt. Bradley and Det. Rosen should be commended for their efforts in allaying the anxieties of our staff at South Beach Psychiatric Center by being open and candid in instructing them on police procedures regarding summons, arrests, etc.

Very truly yours,

James J. Mahoney (b)
James J. Mahoney
Director, Facility Administrative Services

JJM:fb

144

Chapter Thirteen

A resident of Oakwood Beach, Staten Island was walking along the beach on September 18, 1981 when he discovered the badly decomposed and shark-eaten body of a man who had washed ashore. Though this man had no identification, he was wearing dark pants and a gold bracelet with the name "Irving" written in diamonds. He was gagged with a tie wrapped around his mouth and head. Charles Amam had been walking on the beach with his daughter when he came upon the body at the foot of Kissam Ave., Oakwood. Cause of death could not be immediately determined due to the advanced state of decomposition, however, I and the other detectives at the scene ruled out robbery as a motive. In addition to the diamond bracelet, other jewelry – including an expensive watch stopped at September 4th, were still on the body. The body was taken to the Medical Examiner's office in Manhattan.

The decomposed body was later identified by a relative as that of Irving Bitz, a convicted labor racketeer from Medford, Long Island. My investigation of the victim's background uncovered a remarkable history of involvement with organized crime.

Arrested for firearms violations in 1922 and 1931 and a narcotics violation in 1926, Bitz's notoriety in criminal activity began with the kidnapping case of Charles A. Lindbergh's infant son. The Lindbergh baby had been taken from the nursery of the family home in Hopewell, New Jersey by unknown persons who were demanding a ransom. Lindbergh reached out to mob

boss "Lucky" Luciano for assistance, and he assigned Salvatore
("Salvy") Spitale and Irving Bitz as the go-betweens between
the Luciano mob and the Lindbergh family. Colonel Lindbergh
and his wife – the former Anne Morrow, signed a message to the
kidnappers as negotiations for the child's recovery. Bitz circulated
between nightclubs and speakeasies, hoping to pick up information
about who had snatched the baby. Bitz was later referred to as
"Lindbergh's personal emissary".

Despite radio pleas by churches, when leaders of three faiths
offered sanctuary for the child and safety for the abductors, the
exchange was never successfully completed, and the baby was later
discovered dead.

In early May, 1929, the Jewish-American crime boss, Meyer
Lansky was married in Atlantic City. The honeymoon location was
determined to be an ideal place for Lansky to mix business with
pleasure, so a conference was set up there, with mob bosses from
all over the United States invited. Discussed at this conference
were ways of offsetting the mob's loss of profits from the end of
Prohibition, as well as discussions about dividing the country into
exclusive franchises and territories for the bosses. Legitimate liquor
business and gambling figured prominently in these discussions.

From New York/New Jersey were: John "The Fox" Torrio,
former Capone Gang boss, Charles "Lucky" Luciano, Frank "The
Prime Minister" Costello and Vito Genovese, all of the Masseria
Family, and Frank Scalise and Albert Anastasia of the D'Aquila/
Mineo Family, among others.

Representing Chicago were: Alphonse "Scarface" Capone,
Frank "The Enforcer" Nitti and others from the South Side/
Capone Gang, Gaetano "Tommy Brown" Lucchese of the Riena
family, Meyer "The Brain" Lansky and Benjamin "Bugsy" Siegal
of the Bugs and Meyer Mob, Louis Buchalter and Jacob Shapiro
of the Buchalter/Shapiro Gang, Dutch Schultz, Gang Boss,
and others.

From Philadelphia were: Jewish Mob bosses Waxey Gordon,
Max Hoff, Harry Stromberg, Charles Schwartz, Samuel Lazar, and
Irving Bitz, before he moved up to New York.

Cleveland, Detroit (the Purple Gang, all Jews), Kansas City, New England, Louisiana and Florida (Santo Trafficante, Sr.) were also represented.

Bitz had relationships over the decades with many of these and other noted mob bosses, and was known to have been influential in keeping the peace among mob factions, who nicknamed him "The Little Guy" because of his diminutive stature. He was a feisty businessman who was the prime suspect in the 1931 slaying of the famed gambler, Jack "Legs" Diamond, reportedly under orders from a rival bootlegger, Arthur Flegenheimer, known as "Dutch Schultz". Diamond had had three previously unsuccessful attempts on his life, one of them at a restaurant in the Catskills, owned by the brother of "Salvy" Spitale.

Early in his criminal career Bitz was a known associate of Charles "Lucky" Luciano, identified as the "capo di tutti capi" (boss of all bosses) in the Cosa Nostra. Later, Bitz became a close associate of the mob's financial wizard, Meyer Lansky. In more recent years Bitz had reportedly been close with Frank "Funzi" Tieri, who ran the Vito Genovese crime family. They reportedly had a regular meeting each Sunday, with Bitz driving from his Medford, Long Island home to Tieri's house in Brooklyn, to breakfast on bagels and cream cheese, until Tieri's death, earlier this year. Of the other charges Bitz faced, were the bail-jumping violation in 1936 and the 1959 conspiracy and racketeering charges, for which Bitz admitted his guilt.

Bitz was last seen alive when he left his home on the morning of September 2, 1981. When he failed to return home that evening, his fiancé, Sylvia Eisenberg, 71, reported him missing. Later that morning Bitz called his office at the Imperial News Company in Melville, and asked the president, David Liebowitz to prepare a package with $150,000. Bitz's relationship with the Imperial News Company was that he ran the union which controlled all the newspaper delivery trucks.

An armed guard brought the money to Liebowitz and the package was prepared early that afternoon, and an anonymous man called and ordered that the package be delivered to a car parked in front of a doughnut shop on Route 110. An employee of the news delivery firm, Ralph Scarsella reportedly dropped the package into the empty car. Scarsella then checked himself into a hospital that afternoon, complaining of a heart ailment, so we had difficulty questioning him.

At the time of his death, Bitz was 78 years old, and was the last of the Prohibition-era gangsters, and the last surviving member of Murder Incorporated, responsible for over 1,000 killings in the 1930's. His ending was (perhaps fittingly) done brutally – gangland-style – with both legs broken before he was strangled. During his years in the rackets, Bitz served more than 15 years in lockup, but managed to avoid arrest after 1959.

On the day of his abduction, Bitz was heading from Long Island to the City for a certified copy of his late wife's death certificate, so that he could marry Sylvia Eisenberg. I had been assigned the case after Suffolk County officials confirmed that the body was found on Staten Island, and would be investigated by the Crimes Against Persons Squad. Initially the Coast Guard indicated that the murder may have occurred in Brooklyn or New Jersey.

His automobile was recovered at the long-term parking section at Kennedy Airport. Working with the Coast Guard, it was determined that he was dumped into Jamaica Bay, and that the tides had brought his body over to Staten Island, where he washed ashore.

I attempted to interview Ralph Scarsella, who had been the last person to handle the ransom money, and he became the prime suspect in the case. However, Scarsella had moved to Florida, and I was unable to receive any assistance from law enforcement there, as the Organized Crime Task Force had not yet been developed. Unfortunately, I wasn't able to accumulate enough probable cause to affect an arrest.

I worked diligently on this case, but it was never solved.

Chapter Fourteen

On the night of Thursday, October 22, 1981, Salvatore Marisca, 19, was finally arrested as he tried to flee from his mother's house at 101 Regis Drive in his underwear. The police had received a call alerting us to the suspect's location. When Detective Paul DiStefano and I arrived at the home at 10:40 pm, Marisca attempted to elude capture by exiting the house through a rear window. He was accused of robbing and raping a 36 year old barmaid in a Grant City tavern on July 14, 1981 and had reportedly been in hiding in New Jersey since the incident.

I ran around to the back of the house, scaling a six foot fence in my pursuit of the suspect, while DiStefano ran down Regis Drive in an attempt to block the suspect's escape. We did lose Marisca temporarily, but were joined in the hunt by officers from the 122nd Precinct. Officer Robert Bollen of the 122 heard noises coming from a shed at 100 Regis Drive and discovered the suspect inside the shed, pulling on a pair of pants. He must have grabbed his pants as he fled out the window.

On the night of the crimes he committed, Marisca was the last patron at the bar where the victim worked. As barmaid, she had been gathering the night's receipts when the suspect allegedly put a knife to her throat. Following forty minutes of robbing and raping the woman, Marisca allegedly fled from the bar, escaping in the victim's car.

Marisca was accused of robbery, rape, sodomy, grand larceny of an automobile, possession of a weapon and unlawful imprisonment. He was also wanted on a robbery charge by authorities in Florida, whom we notified. Marisca was found guilty, did time in New York, then was extradited to Florida to face the charges against him in that state.

At 3:30 pm on the afternoon of Friday, November 27, 1981 five men shot Fred Rogers, 23, near his home at 29 Warren St., Stapleton, Staten Island. They then abducted him and transported him by car to Travis, where they dumped his body in a secluded field near South Ave. and Chelsea Rd. about an hour later. But they weren't yet done with Rogers, whom they shot several times more, leaving him for dead. In all, a pistol and a shotgun were used to shoot the victim seven times.

A motorist who was driving along Chelsea Rd., heading to Francesco's, a local salvage yard. He heard Rogers' cries for help and picked up Ben Francesco, the operator of the yard. They rushed back to discover Rogers and the victim was taken to St. Vincent's Medical Center, where he underwent surgery and was listed in stable, but guarded condition.

I was assigned to investigate, with Detective Paul Frommer, also of the Crimes Against Persons Squad. Following numerous leads, we were able to determine that the crime was likely one of mistaken identity. Without definite identification of the attackers, it seemed that they mistook Rogers (an apparent look-alike) for an associate in a drug deal. Rogers was an innocent bystander with no criminal record, who was apparently shot and grabbed by mistake.

Canvassing of both locations came up with negative results. We offered to give Rogers a chance to come into the precinct, following his release from the hospital to look at mug shots. Unfortunately, Rogers told us that he was unable to identify the shooters.

Christmas 1981 was a heartbreaker.

Paul Frommer and I, as Jewish cops, volunteered to work Christmas Eve and Christmas Day, so that cops of Christian faith could celebrate the holiday with their families.

Detective Frommer and I were sent out to investigate an Aided Case (D.O.A) at a home on December 24th during our evening (4pm - 1am) shift. We arrived to find a young couple who was devastated over the loss of their first child, who had just been discovered unconscious and not breathing. I examined the body for any signs of physical abuse. The cause of the infant's death was determined as S.I.D.S. (sudden infant death syndrome), also referred to as "crib death".

This was to have been the child's first Christmas. The Christmas tree in their home was lit and beautifully decorated, laden beneath with wrapped gifts. Both Paul and I were so saddened by this, which was to have been a day of joyous celebration for the family. Nonetheless, we covered the next day's 8am - 4pm Christmas Day detail.

Three days later 20-year-old Roy Johnson was in an argument with another man in the courtyard of 806 Henderson Ave. at the West Brighton Houses complex on Monday, December 28, 1981. The man Johnson argued with was accompanied by another man who walked behind Johnson and stabbed him once in the upper left side of his back. The single thrust proved fatal.

Before he died, the victim staggered around the building to a ground floor apartment at 780 Henderson Ave. to summon help. When an ambulance arrived to take him to St. Vincent's Medical Center, Johnson was unconscious. He was pronounced D.O.A. (dead on arrival) when he reached the hospital.

Investigating the murder, it wasn't initially clear why a man so badly hurt would stumble so far for help, instead of entering the nearby building. We were unable to locate the occupant of the building Johnson had gone to, where he was stabbed.

We canvassed the area, discovering that a number of other people had formed a modest crowd around Johnson and the man he had been arguing with. At some point Johnson had reportedly thrown a beer bottle in anger, before being stabbed from behind. We had a suspect whom we wanted to question for the stabbing, and police units were on the lookout for him.

Some two months later, William Browne, 20, surrendered to my partner, Detective Catherine Bertolino. Browne, the suspect we'd sought, entered the 122nd Precinct stationhouse in New Dorp between 4 and 5 pm to turn himself in. He was then taken to the 120th Precinct (Central Booking) in St. George, where he was held until his scheduled arraignment the next morning in Stapleton Criminal Court.

Chapter Fifteen

January 1982 began with a spate of crimes that I was assigned to investigate.

The first such crime was on Friday, January 8th, when a lone gunman robbed a Chase Manhattan Bank in Port Richmond. The robber reportedly entered the bank armed with a revolver, forcing three tellers to empty their cash drawers at gunpoint. After grabbing an undisclosed amount of cash, it was reported that he raced out of the branch bank at 26 Richmond Avenue a little before noon.

During my investigation of the robbery, witnesses told me that the thief ran along Richmond Ave. toward Church Street, but provided few additional clues. This ended as an unresolved case...

During the very next week, Wednesday, January 13, 1982, a gunman robbed a gas station in Port Richmond, escaping with some $2000.

Employees Ralph Tulloch and Joseph Rivera were working that evening at the Exxon station at 2239 Forest Avenue. Rivera was inside the station, while Tulloch was working outside, pumping gas. Once the last customer pulled out, Tulloch returned to the office to find a stranger on the telephone. As Tulloch walked by, the assailant put his hand on Tulloch's shoulder and stuck a pistol to his ribs.

The robber then locked both Tulloch and Rivera in the gas station's bathroom before escaping with the money. There were no other witnesses to this robbery, so this, too, became an unresolved case.

Late the following Saturday night presented an interesting discovery. Detectives, assisting uniformed police, rushed to the aid of a Willowbrook couple that had reportedly been taken hostage in their home, and we uncovered a major narcotics operation.

At about 11pm on that Saturday, Police Officers John Sellenthin and Joseph Dessoye were sent to a house at 76 Golfer Place, from which police had received a report of a possible hostage situation. Upon arrival at this address, the officers found Anthony Suarrci, 24, of that address. Locked outside the house, Suarrci said that someone was holding his wife hostage inside.

Just then, Suarrci's wife Geraldine, also 24, threw a set of keys out a second story window, calling for help. Unable to find a key for the front door, the officers were able to enter the house through the garage. When they'd made their way upstairs, they found Mrs. Suarrci safe. Searching for the man who'd reportedly held her hostage, we found no other persons were found in the house.

However, there was quite a bit else discovered: at least $40,000 worth of various drugs and three guns were found on the premises. As the Suarrci couple was arrested, more than four ounces of pure cocaine was confiscated, several pounds of white powder (presumably used to "cut" the coke), and approximately seven pounds of marijuana.

As this was a weekend, I obtained a search warrant from Supreme Court Justice Norman Felig, who signed it at his home. Returning to the scene of the crime, post-arrest, our subsequent search uncovered a pharmaceutical bottle, containing 5000 Secanol pills, valued at $5 each, as well as additional marijuana and white powder. We sent this batch of powder to the lab for analysis, suspecting it was also meant to be used to dilute the pure cocaine.

~

In early 1982 I arrested a man on Puerto Rico's 10 Most Wanted list.

William Gordon Pagan was convicted in 1976 of the shooting death of Jose Antonio Burges Alicia in Ponce, Puerto Rico. He's been serving a life sentence for First Degree Murder at the Rio Piedras State Penitentiary, and was also serving time for a previous escape from jail. He and four other inmates escaped from Rio Piedras on December 3, 1981. Gordon fled Puerto Rico and took up residence in Staten Island.

Acting on a confidential tip, I arrested Gordon Pagan, who offered no resistance, at 3355 Hylan Blvd. A rifle, some marijuana, a revolver that had been robbed from a policeman and a stolen car were seized. After he was arrested and processed, in a cell waiting to go before a judge, he offered me a key (kilo) of cocaine to let him off the hook. Of course I declined the offer, but as he was already in the system, it made no sense to hold up his prosecution by adding attempted bribery to his charges.

I had been communicating with police authorities from Puerto Rico, and Pedro M. Roman of The San Juan Star sent me articles about this murderer from his newspaper, printed in both Spanish and English.

The Puerto Rican Justice Department's Attorney, Roberto Buono Grillasca filed for extradition of Gordon Pagan. The prisoner chose not to fight the extradition orders and was returned to Puerto Rico.

Chapter Sixteen

June 10-11, 1982

At the beginning of the book you read part of a case, entitled June 11, 1982. The story began on the evening before and will now be told in greater detail.

For clarification, the following is a list of the New York City Police Department personnel at that time, who became involved in this case:

- Deputy Chief-Richard NiCastro
  - *Borough Commander*
- Deputy Inspector-Daniel O'Brien
  - *In charge of all Detectives on Staten Island*
- Lt. William Quinn-Commanding Officer
  - *Crimes Against Persons Squad*
- Sgt. Patrick Bradley-Supervisor of Team C
  - *Crimes Against Persons Squad, which consisted*
    of 6 Detectives

On the Dates of Incident, my partner for that tour of duty was Detective Robert Fahey.

Team C was performing a 4pm - 1am Tour of Duty.

Fahey was a Member of the S. I. Street Crime Unit. When that Unit was dissolved late in 1980, Fahey and several other

Members of that Unit were reassigned to the Crimes Against Persons Squad.

There were no steady partners in the Detective Squad. This afforded me the opportunity to work with a number of detectives on the team. Several squad members were native Staten Islanders, while the rest, like myself, were transplants from various squads in Manhattan and Brooklyn.

My partner in this investigation, Bob Fahey, was a native of Staten Island, whom I genuinely enjoyed working with. During our tours together, he'd tell me about the history of Staten Island before the Verrazano Bridge was built in 1964. Bob knew the Island like the back of his hand, showing me sidewalks in the middle of a forest in Tottenville, explaining that they'd been built during the 1930s by the WPA. While the country was surviving the Great Depression, Roosevelt's WPA provided such construction jobs to the unemployed. When Fahey and I were conducting investigations, Bob pointed out places of interest to me, like the location of Anti-Aircraft Artillery placed on the Island during WWII. He also took me on a personal tour of Fort Wadsworth, across the bay from Fort Hamilton in Brooklyn.

Fahey was a good family man of Catholic faith, and looked like a typical Irish-American cop. I took him to a Kosher Deli one night for dinner. The place was noted for having a New York City subway car in the middle of the dining room where patrons could sit and eat. When the waiter came to take our order, Bob asked for a kielbasa sandwich and a glass of milk. The waiter looked at me, and I had to explain to Fahey that what he'd ordered was not Kosher – no pork, and no milk with meat. I suggested the corned beef sandwich on rye with a soda, and a knish to go with it. This was his first experience with Jewish food and he enjoyed it immensely.

To this day we have remained friends, and we stay in contact on a monthly basis via phone. One of the best partners I ever worked with, he'll call me every Jewish New Year, and I reciprocate a call to him every Christmas Day.

Robert Fahey was a highly decorated cop, who had been involved in three prior justified shootings. He was awarded approximately 56 medals, including Combat Crosses, numerous Commendations, and Meritorious Police Duty and Excellent Police Duty awards.

On June 10, 1982 at 11pm, I left the station house with Sergeant Bradley and Detective Fahey to answer a call. The Squad had been notified of a stabbing at Bayley Seton Hospital, and we were going to interview the victim. We found him being treated at the hospital in stable condition, but we were unable to interview further, as he was receiving medical attention. While at the hospital, a signal 10-13 came over the radio – which we heard between 11:30 and 11:45pm. Such a call always puts a stop to whatever else is happening, but this call proved unfounded.

At the hospital, we received a call from the Squad, where we learned of – and immediately responded to – a kidnapping (between 11:30 - 12 midnight). We proceeded to Acme Supermarket on Marsh Ave., with the drive taking approximately 15 minutes. When we arrived at 12:10 am, there were Detectives Wilke and Petraglia already at the scene, requesting assistance.

Two perpetrators wearing ski masks had reportedly kidnapped the Acme store manager from the parking lot. The manager had reportedly entered his car to leave the lot, when another vehicle cut his car off and forced him at gunpoint into their vehicle, described as a medium sized car, possibly light colored.

This much we learned in 5-10 minutes from a witness, who we placed in the squad car to accompany us on our search of the mall's immense parking lot. We stopped our car at Platinum Avenue, when we saw an old, beat-up, light colored car with a man inside. The guy was a Security Guard for Foxwood Square. We were disappointed that he wasn't able to enlighten us with a further account which he may have seen, so we drove the witness passenger back to Acme.

Sgt. Bradley then ordered Fahey and me to search the Travis area, in an attempt to locate the kidnapped victim. Several months before, there had been an earlier Acme Manager kidnapping, and the manager had been found in Travis. It was almost 12:30 am when we began our search.

Within 15 minutes we observed a vehicle occupied by two males parked in the opposite direction on Bridge Street. We passed, made a U-turn and came up behind the vehicle. I approached the driver's side and identified myself – shield in hand. The car's occupants were eating sandwiches and drinking beverages. I asked the driver for his license and registration, which he produced. After checking the car's license plate, I asked the two in the car if they'd seen anything unusual, to which they answered no. I then gave the driver back his license and registration and told them to have a good night. It was now approaching 12:45am.

We then traveled on the northbound service road of the West Shore Expressway until we reached its end, getting on the Expressway itself, northbound, for less than a mile, where we exited onto the service road for the Staten Island Expressway, eastbound.

I was set to make a right-hand turn at South Ave., intending to head back toward Victory Blvd., when Fahey asked me to make a left, so that we could check out the dumping area on the other side of the Expressway. He told me that safes and other contraband had previously been found there. From South Avenue, I made another left turn onto Goethals Road North, a road with two lanes heading in the same direction, beneath the elevated Staten Island Expressway. Some 500 feet after making the turn, we observed a light-colored vehicle parked on the right side of the road. Just off the right side of the road the green of heavy vegetation ran alongside, with telephone poles equipped with lights atop them.

I'd traveled this road a number of times before, finding abandoned, stripped automobiles there. I was now driving slowly – no more than 5 mph, with my high beams on as we approached the parked vehicle.

I stopped the unmarked car directly behind the vehicle that was parked in the dark on the right side of the road. My headlights' high beams shined through the other car's rear window and out through its windshield, indicating an empty automobile. So I pulled alongside the parked car, with my partner, Detective Fahey in the passenger seat.

A man jumped up and came out of the other vehicle, shouting, "What the fuck you doin'?"

Suddenly, our passenger side window exploded loudly. I turned to see blood shooting out from Bobby Fahey's face, before he brought his hands to his face, and the blood continued to spurt out between his fingers.

"I'm shot, Gary!" he cried, leaning forward.

Bobby somehow managed to stick his right arm out the opening where the window had been, and he fired a shot.

I swung out of the driver's door with my 6-shot Colt Detective Special revolver in my hand, moving quickly around the back of the car. The assailant was upon me before I could clearly see him, attacking me with a club-like weapon at the rear of the car. This guy, about 6' 2" and 220 pounds, towered over my 5' 11", 165 pound frame. With my free hand, I grabbed the guy by the arm that held the club, and brought the full force of my handgun down on his head with my other hand. As he fell, I could see that he was wearing a red shirt but was otherwise naked. He attempted to get up a second time, so I struck him again.

The son-of-a-bitch actually tried coming at me again, but I didn't realize that he'd already taken a bullet through his heart, lung and liver. I clocked him a third time, knocking him down. This time my blow to his head felled him hard. He was never to get up again.

I called in a 10-13: Officer Down.

I requesting an ambulance to Goethals Road North which was a service road for the Staten Island Expressway. Then a woman came out of the parked car's passenger side, shouting in my direction. She was nude, covering the front of her body with articles of clothing she was holding.

"Get back in the car," I told her.

A patrol car arrived before the ambulance, so I put Bobby in the patrol car and had the responding officers take him to the hospital. Checking the attacker's pulse, I noted that he was still alive, grunting on the ground. I told him to stay calm, and that an ambulance was on its way. Other patrol cars arrived immediately, but I remained at the scene for several hours, as other police units arrived.

Meanwhile, the female kept screaming at me, calling me a "scumbag cop". When Sergeant Bradley arrived at the scene I told him what had happened. A search of the car was made before it was impounded, and the police recovered a number of items from the auto. Among them were nitrous oxide cartridges, and a device designed to open the cartridges – ostensibly for filling balloons – but also allowing the gas to be inhaled by humans. Nitrous oxide had been used by some people who believed that it enhanced sexual relations.

Eventually, Lieutenant Quinn also responded to the scene and later transported me back to the Squad, where I spoke with a union representative from the D.E.A. (Detectives Endowment Association).

The names of the two people in that car were Anthony Ruggierio and Debbie Boyd. Ruggierio was pronounced D.O.A. at the scene, while being administered medical assistance.

There was a Department Hearing at the stationhouse at 8 am that morning of June 11, 1982. In attendance were Deputy Chief NiCastro, Deputy Inspector Daniel O'Brian, Captain McGivny, A.D.A., William Fredricks of the Staten Island D.A.'s office, and D.E.A. Attorney Mr. Panatella. Deputy Inspector O'Brian produced the weapon Ruggierio had used in his attack on me and Fahey. It was a wood piece, some 12 inches long. One end had a rubber knob. From the other end protruded a chrome cylinder, the diameter of a 12 gauge shotgun barrel. This was apparently the base for a deep sea, heavy fishing rod, which would be locked into the chrome cylinder.

Detective Fahey returned to the Squad from the hospital some time in the early morning. He still appeared to be in shock. There were numerous cuts around his face and he seemed depressed. At some point, between 11 am and noon, we finally went home.

Although this was finally the end of a hellish night, the trauma of what had happened during that fateful shift was to have a devastating effect on a number of individuals, especially Bob Fahey and me.

An autopsy performed on Ruggierio noted that the cause of death was one bullet hole through the heart, lung and liver. His blood contained nitrous oxide as well as narcotics – believed to have been ingested with the intention of enhancing a sexual climax.

Anthony Ruggierio's father, Donato Ruggierio was a Captain of the Supreme Court Officers for Brooklyn. The father, who carried a gun, went to the Brooklyn District Attorney's office, meeting with then-Brooklyn D.A. Elizabeth Holtzman to pressure her to take an active role. Ms. Holtzman telephoned the Staten Island D.A., Thomas Sullivan to review the case.

Demonstrations in front of the Staten Island D.A.'s office building on Richmond Terrace, organized by Ruggierio's family members, began and increased in frequency. Anthony Ruggierio's fiancé was photographed at one such demonstration published in the Staten Island Advance, holding a sign that read "I Can't Wed Because They Shot Anthony Dead."

Fahey and I had received numerous death threats delivered via phone calls to the squad office. We filed a case with the threat desk of the NYPD Intelligence Unit. As a result, we were offered 24-hour coverage, with patrol cars to sit in front of our residences. We declined this offer and opted for take-home police department radios.

Investigations were begun into the shooting, conducted by the following units and agencies: Crimes Against Persons Squad, Staten Island D.A.'s Squad, and the Internal Affairs Unit (spearheaded by Staten Island Field Internal Affairs Unit). Without confirmation, it was believed that the F.B.I. – part of the Department of Justice – along with the U.S. Attorney's Office were investigating for Violation of Civil Rights.

A Richmond County grand jury (Staten Island) was impaneled to investigate the shooting. Both Fahey and I were required to testify and we both waived our immunity. The grand jury result was that there was no "bill" (indictment). They found the shooting to be justified.

Before the investigations were too far underway, I was called into the office of the Borough Commander, Deputy Chief Richard NiCastro for a one-on-one informal meeting. NiCastro opened by telling me that he had read my department evaluations, and noted that I had been recommended for promotion to 2nd Grade Detective.

He then asked me, "Off the record, what really happened?"

I simply told him to read the DD5s, an answer which didn't seem to satisfy him. I followed up by telling him that if he wanted to question me further, I would have wanted a D.E.A. attorney present. Without missing a beat, I turned and walked out of his office. He never questioned me again.

The death threats to Fahey and me continued. Rumors surfaced that Ruggierio's father had personal plans of hurting us both. The rumors could not be substantiated, but may have influenced the reported request by the Staten Island D.A.'s office to the Brooklyn D.A.'s office that Ruggierio have his gun removed from him. Ultimately, Donato Ruggierio was allowed to keep his hand gun.

While we were conducting another investigation, Fahey and I were at Police Headquarters at 1 Police Plaza picking up some reports and photos. There, we saw the Commanding Officer of the Staten Island Field Internal Affairs Unit, Captain Henry Sabernick, talking outside of Chief Guido's office, the Commanding Officer of the Internal Affairs Division. Sabernick saw us, too.

That day as we were completing our 8-4 shift, and members of the 4-1 shift were coming into the squad room, I saw Sabernick enter the squad room. Bobby was in the back locker room at that moment. In front of the accumulated police present, Sabernick pointed his finger at me and stated: "I was just with Chief Guido, and I'm going to lock you and Fahey up for murder," as he turned and left the squad room. Present to witness Sabernick's confrontation of me were: the Squad Commander, Lieutenant Quinn, Sergeant Bradley, and another Sergeant and the Detectives from both the day and evening shifts. I asked Lt. Quinn if he knew about Sabernick's statement. Quinn answered no, telling me that he was going to find out what was going on. I mentioned that Fahey and I had seen Sabernick talking with Chief Guido.

Since this was our last day-duty shift, Quinn told me to get Fahey and go home. We were going on a swing, with regular days off. When I went to the locker room and told Fahey, he was mortified. We left the station house together, heading home.

The next day I received a phone call from Lt. Quinn. He told me that he'd spoken with Sabernick, who told Quinn he was "only joking". Some joke! Sabernick's open confrontation occurred several months after the shooting. I called Bobby Fahey and brought him up-to-date.

When I returned to work for my first 4-1 shift I spoke with Lt. Quinn, practicing the respect of going through the chain of command. I told him that I was still very upset about the incident with Capt. Sabernick and that I'd come up with an idea on how to retaliate against him. I asked Lt. Quinn if a cop could make a Civilian Complaint against another member of the force. Lt. Quinn stated that he didn't know and had never heard about any cop who'd ever done that. Lt. Quinn advised me to see the Desk Officer of the 122nd Pct. about making a Civilian Complaint. Lt. Quinn then gave me his blessing.

I went downstairs. The Desk Officer on duty was an old time Irish Lt. who had a heavy brogue. He said: "What could I do for you, Laddie?", knowing I was a detective from the squad. I asked him if a cop could make a Civilian Complaint against another cop. He looked at me with a bewildered expression, telling me that he didn't know if CCRB would take the complaint. He asked me who the complaint would be against. When I told him it was Capt. Sabernick, a big smile ran across his face. Then he said "fuck that scumbag" and gave me the CCRB (Civilian Complaint Review Board) forms for me to fill out. I went back up to the squad room.

I filled out the paperwork starting with what Capt. Sabernick had said to me. Out of respect to Lt. Quinn, I showed him the complaint I was filing. He stated "go for it". So, I went back to the lieutenant on the desk and handed him my complaint. He called CCRB who took the complaint and assigned a case number to it. CCRB told the lieutenant that something like this had never been done in the entire history of the department. I was thrilled that CCRB took the case. It's not often when you could fuck an Internal Affairs Captain.

Upon arriving for my first 4-1 shift the following week I was told to go to the Borough office and report to Deputy Chief SanMarino, who was now the Borough Commander. CCRB kicked my complaint back to the Borough for investigation by the Chief.

I proceeded to the Borough Office, not having previously met the Chief, but knowing that he had a son who'd been on the job for several years. Entering the Chief's office, I saw Chief SanMarino already rubbing his face, as if to soothe a headache. I formally introduced myself and the Chief asked me, "How I did I get stuck with this bucket of shit?" I related the incident when Sabernick told me that he was going to arrest me and Fahey for murder.

I then asked the Chief, "You have a son that's on he job. How would you feel, if some Captain said that to him?"

The Chief assured me that Fahey and I were not going to be arrested, and that he was unaware of any further investigation of us. When I reported that Lt. Quinn had been told by Sabernick that he was only joking, the Chief asked me what I thought should be Sabernick's discipline.

I said, "Flop him back into uniform."

The Chief said no to this suggestion, asking me to come up with another idea. I thought about alternatives, and settled on asking Sabernick to come into the squad room and make a public apology in front of me, Fahey and everyone who was present when he'd made his untrue and outrageous statement. The Chief said that sounded fair, adding that if Sabernick refused to make this public apology, he would take away Sabernick's command and put him back in uniform. I asked for Sabernick to make his apology on my last day-tour, while all those who were initially present would be there, requesting that it be done at 3:55 pm, the time of shift change.

On my last day-tour, at exactly 3:55 pm Captain Sabernick entered the squad room. Despite his squeamish presentation, Sabernick spoke in a loud voice, announcing his apology to me and Fahey. He stated that it was stupid of him to have made such a statement, and that there had been no truth to it. An unknown Detective in the back of the room called him an asshole, prompting laughter from everyone there. With that, Sabernick sheepishly left the room. He never bothered me again.

Fahey and I were on our days off. Unbeknownst to me, Bobby went shopping alone at the indoor Victory Flea Market where he was approached by a white female who asked him if he was Bob Fahey. Fahey, a bit surprised, answered "Yes". The woman then told him that Fahey's kids will be killed, "and their blood will run through the streets, like my brother's".

Bobby, reeling in shock, suddenly felt sick to the point of practically passing out. He made it to the security office, where they notified the Squad. Members rushed to the scene, securing Fahey for his safety. The woman who'd accosted Bobby was indeed identified as Ruggierio's sister.

I was called, told what had happened, and advised that Fahey was being taken to the Squad Room, where I rushed to be with him. It was apparent that he was in emotional and mental distress, but didn't wish to go to the hospital. Paramedics came to the Squad Room to check Fahey out. Bobby was treated on-site for elevated blood pressure and stress.

The NYPD Employee Relations Unit was called, and Sgt. Luby from that unit responded to the Squad Room from Manhattan. Fahey again refused hospitalization. When I looked into his eyes there was a recognition that he had had enough of the job. A great cop had reached his breaking point. Again, the department offered to have a patrol car assigned to his residence. Fahey again declined.

Employee Relations' Sergeant Luby took a tremendous personal interest in Fahey's welfare, paving the way for an unobstructed pathway to Fahey's retirement. He wound up retiring in February of 1984. Several years later I made contact with Sgt. Luby, who assisted me on my disability retirement, which resulted from an old injury sustained in the line of duty.

There were two dates during which I was required to give depositions: June 20, 1984 and June 28, 1984. For both of these occasions I was asked a series of questions by Ruggierio's attorney. These were, in effect, examinations before trial, held at the

Brooklyn Federal Courthouse, Eastern District at 225 Cadman Place, Brooklyn, N.Y.

We were being sued in Federal Court by Ruggierio's family under Statute 1983, Violation of Civil Rights Under the Color of Law. Overseeing these procedures was Judge Jack Weinstein who had gained notoriety when he'd overseen the highly publicized Agent Orange trial.

Fahey and I were represented by the City of New York Corporation Counsel. We were both indemnified because we had not violated any rules and procedures of the NYPD Patrol Guide and there was no criminal action.

The Corporation Counsel arranged an agreement with Ruggierio's attorneys: there would be no mention to the jury of Anthony Ruggierio's drugs, and no mention of Bobby Fahey's prior – and justified – shootings.

The trial itself took place in 1988. By that time I'd retired and had moved down to Florida. New York City paid all my expenses to fly me up to be present at the trial. The City of New York had originally offered the Ruggierio family a $250,000 non-prejudicial settlement, but the family declined this offer and opted for a jury trial.

The results of the trial before jury were that Anthony Ruggierio was found 33.3% negligent, for his actions against the police, Robert Fahey was found 33.3% negligent, for the shooting of Ruggierio, and I, Gary Rosen was found 33.3% negligent, for not restraining Fahey from shooting Ruggierio. The final result was that the Ruggierio family was compensated $100,000, plus $6,000 for funeral expenses.

Six long years after that horrific night the courts placed a stamp of finality on the incident.

Police lead James DiGuglielmo, suspected in the murder of Robert Nagengast, out of the 120th Precinct stationhouse, St. George.
S.I. Advance Photo by Frank J. Johns

Man, 23, is indicted in beating, drowning

A one-count murder indictment was filed yesterday against James DiGuglielmo, 23, who is accused of beating and drowning Robert Nagengast of Port Richmond.

The defendant, of 99 Memphis Ave., Eltingville, has been held without bail since Wednesday. He was ordered to appear for arraignment next Friday in Supreme Court, St. George.

The indictment accuses him of murder in the second degree and sets time of the incident as "on or about July 8."

Nagengast, a 22-year-old bartender in Artie's Tavern, Port Richmond, was found floating off a Stapleton pier in the Upper Bay on Monday morning.

The suspect was identified by police as an unemployed steel worker.

In other court action yesterday, John Luczun of 23 Herkimer St., West Brighton, was indicted on six counts of possessing stolen property.

Luczun, 26, allegedly had several typewriters and copying machines at his house that belonged to other persons, six of whom are listed in the indictment.

He was arrested in March.

Dane Smith, 17, of 118 Bloomingdale Rd., Charleston, was accused of burglary and criminal mischief.

An indictment charges that he vandalized a classroom at Our Lady Star of the Sea School, 5411 Amboy Rd., Huguenot, in January.

In addition, burglary and criminal mischief charges were filed against two teen-agers who allegedly cut a screen at a residence in their neighborhood, at Flagg Pl., Dongan Hills.

Gary Heintz, 18, of 120 Vista Ave., and Joseph Kent, 17, of 51 Dongan Hills Ave., both Dongan Hills, are accused committing the crimes on or about May 3.

Felony charges were also filed, by the district attorney's office, against James Celentano, 46, of Sunnyside, who was accused of operating a motor vehicle under the influence of alcohol on May 25.

from Staten Island Advance

Chapter Seventeen

Early on the morning of Wednesday, August 11, 1982, a man from New Brighton was stabbed in the abdomen while walking near Tappen Park in Stapleton.

Kenneth Brailford, 25, was taken to Bayley Seton Hospital with a serious wound to his midsection. Fortunately, the knife he was stabbed with somehow missed all of the victim's vital organs. Brailford had been walking when an assailant approached him suddenly from behind at the intersection of Wright and Canal Streets. The one knife thrust was the extent of the attack.

I was unable to learn more information in the hope of identifying a motive or a suspect in this case.

A couple of weeks later, I did have success with the investigation of an unrelated robbery. On August 26, 1982, I arrested Mabel Norman, 27, in Tompkinsville, as she stood at the intersection of Bay and Grant Streets. She was charged with the robbery of a 30 year old Clifton man on the previous Sunday.

It had been at 6 am on Sunday, August 22, 1982 that the victim had been walking down the stairway of an apartment at 160 Park Hill Ave. when he was come upon by Ms. Norman and two male suspects, one of whom was armed with a small black revolver. The three assailants robbed the man of $150 in cash and the keys to his 1978 Datsun. After the theft, they locked the victim in a nearby janitor's closet and fled in the stolen car. The two male thieves were still being sought, but Ms. Norman was charged with second degree robbery and grand larceny of an automobile.

Janice Napolitano was an attractive young woman who was known to have frequented drinking establishments. There she would often drink excessively and flirt with a number of men. One of the men she did more than flirt with was James DiGugliemo. He was a very large, well-muscled man, trim and intimidating in his presentation.

On July 7, 1982 Ms. Napolitano confided to the jealous DiGugliemo that another man had "taken advantage" of her two weeks earlier. The man she was referring to was Robert Nagengast, part-time bartender at Artie's Tavern, who had reportedly had sexual relations with Ms. Napolitano, who'd become intoxicated at the bar and had passed out.

The day after Ms. Napolitano's disclosure DiGugliemo was drinking with another young woman at Artie's Tavern. This was Joan Cairo, who worked as a beautician with Ms. Napolitano and was also a frequent patron at Artie's. As the tavern was closing, Ms. Cairo and DiGugliemo decided to go to another bar on Forest Avenue, where they met Nagengast between 3 and 4 am. Although Nagengast had himself been at Artie's earlier that night, he had not been working. The three reportedly decided to buy some beer and go to the Stapleton Pier. Nagengast was never seen or heard from again.

The next day Ms. Cairo called me to express her concerns for Nagengast's well-being, and Detective Jack Timko and I opened an investigation into his disappearance. Ms. Cairo gave me an account of the trio's activities on the night Nagengast went missing. She told me that she had been driving the car, with DiGugliemo and Nagengast as passengers. Cairo was unfamiliar with the location, so the men provided directions to the pier.

Ms. Cairo stated that when they got there, she parked the car and the two men got out, as she waited inside the vehicle. According to Cairo, DiGugliemo returned to the car alone about five minutes later. She stated that DiGugliemo had told her that he'd been in a fight with Nagengast, had "beat him up bad" and had thrown him in the water. She quoted DiGugliemo as saying that "He may be dead."

With no sign of Nagengast, Ms. Cairo told me that she returned to her home, as she was tired from a night of drinking, and that DiGugliemo slept in her home that night.

Later that same day (July 8th), Ms. Cairo saw DiGugliemo again. He reportedly advised her not to "say anything" about what had happened. If anyone should ask – he reportedly coached her – she should tell them that they'd gone to a grocery store to purchase beer, then they'd dropped Nagengast off at his home.

Nagengast's body was found four days later, on July 12, 1982, floating off a Stapleton Pier. His body was badly decomposed. The Medical Examiner's report ruled it as a homicide, cause of death – blunt trauma beating and drowning.

Now, with clarification about the missing Nagengast, Detective Timko and I continued our investigation, and we worked straight through, with no days off. I initiated a BCI check on DiGugliemo, which detailed an extensive history of violent criminal activity.

When I interviewed DiGugliemo on July 13th, he made the same statement that Ms. Cairo had been told by him to make: that the three had gone to a grocery store to purchase beer, then they'd dropped Nagengast off at his home.

Meanwhile, Ms. Napolitano, in fear for her life, fled to the Poconos in Pennsylvania. Ms. Cairo agreed to accompany me and Detective Timko to Pennsylvania, arranging for us to meet with Janice Napolitano. We brought Ms. Napolitano back to New York late that night, actually the early morning of July 14th.

On that day I conferred with Assistant District Attorney Thomas Aliotta, seeking to tap Ms. Napolitano's telephone with her permission. I received the go-ahead and set up a call to DiGugliemo. During the recorded conversation, DiGugliemo pleaded with Ms. Napolitano to contact Ms. Cairo. He said it was "important." DiGugliemo instructed Ms. Napolitano to tell Ms. Cairo to "stick to the story, and everything will be okay." This gave us enough probable cause to make an arrest.

We got a tip about DiGugliemo's whereabouts later that night. Told that he was at a bar, we headed there and arrived to find the place crowded with patrons. Seeing DiGugliemo in a corner of the bar, I approached him quickly and quietly, pointing my gun into his face and placing him under arrest, charging him with murder in the second degree. Instead of bringing my Colt revolver (my off duty gun, with a short, 2" barrel), I used my Smith & Wesson .38 service revolver (used by uniformed officers), which I drew from a shoulder holster. This was a much more intimidating weapon, appropriate to the situation. As noted, DiGugliemo was a big brawler with a long criminal history of assaults and other violent felonies, so I sought to avoid any confrontation in the close confines of that packed establishment.

After his arrest DiGugliemo entered a plea of not guilty and went to trial in January, 1983.

On Tuesday, January 25, 1983 Joan Cairo gave testimony as a witness at the Supreme Court trial. Ms. Cairo testified to what she'd told me when I began the investigation: that she'd driven DiGugliemo and Nagengast to the Stapleton waterfront early on July 8th, where the two men had left her car. She said that only DiGugliemo had returned to the car – without Nagengast.

When questioned about why the two had fought on July 8, 1982, Cairo offered: "Janice, and other reasons." Ms. Cairo testified about the earlier incident when Nagengast, working as a bartender at Artie's Tavern, had allegedly "taken advantage" of a friend after she'd become intoxicated and passed out in the tavern.

DiGugliemo's defense lawyer, David W. Lehr in his opening remarks denied that DiGugliemo, an unemployed steel worker, had "intentionally" caused Nagengast's death. In his cross examination of Ms. Cairo, Lehr asked questions which suggested that she, Cairo had pushed Nagengast from the pier as the men fought. Further, he suggested that Ms. Cairo had been angry about a sexual overture made by Nagengast. Ms. Cairo denied any such conduct.

Testifying further, Cairo said that she did not believe DiGugliemo when he told her that Nagengast might be dead. She testified that she'd believed the two may have been in a fight, and had asked to see where the fight had taken place, to possibly find

Nagengast. Instead, she agreed to return to her home, testifying that DiGugliemo slept in her home that night.

Also giving testimony at the trial was the "Janice" referred to by Ms. Cairo, Janice Napolitano, the beautician who'd worked with Cairo. She told the jury that following the incident involving the two men, Ms. Napolitano had spoken with DiGugliemo and, in fear for her life, had fled to Pennsylvania, from where we had returned her to New York to continue the investigation.

The evidence against DiGugliemo was overwhelming. At the trial's end, the jury found DiGugliemo guilty of second degree murder and he received a long prison sentence.

However, after his conviction, DiGugliemo managed to escape from prison. When he was discovered after his escape and police attempted to re-arrest him, DiGugliemo was shot dead.

The victim, Nagengast, who had been tending bar at Artie's part time at the time of his death, had a history in Port Richmond, where he'd lived all his life. After playing baseball in the Titan League at Blessed Sacrament Roman Catholic Church as a youth, Nagengast attended Susan Wagner High School, before working as a route salesman for Pepsi Cola Co. He was survived by his parents - Peter and Maureen Nagengast, his maternal grandmother - Anne Shaffer, four brothers - Peter, James, Joseph and Edward, and three sisters - Kerry Platz, Tracey Balcombe and Mary Nagengast.

Chapter Eighteen

In the fall of 1982, there was a rash of attacks on women in the Tottenville-Richmond Valley area. Working with Detective Saverio DeMorato, we arrested a young man responsible for a number of rapes on Staten Island.

Patrick Lynch, 21, currently living in Brooklyn with his father, was a former Pleasant Plains resident. He'd been released from Elmira Correctional Facility about a month before, after serving five years for attempted rape. This time, Lynch was arrested for the rape of a 17 year old Richmond Valley girl the previous Friday. We apprehended him on October 5, 1982, when he appeared for a meeting with his probation officer, and charged him with rape, possession of a weapon and unlawful imprisonment.

Lynch had been arrested on September 5, 1977, and charged with the rape of a 15 year old girl on August 8 of that year. He had reportedly threatened the girl with a razor and forced her into the woods near the SIRT station, some 300 feet west of Weiner Street on Richmond Valley Road. He was also charged with the attempted rape and robbery of a Pleasant Plains woman on August 15, 1977, near her home.

After initially having been charged with rape, sodomy, attempted rape, attempted sodomy, two counts of sexual abuse, two counts of robbery and two counts of criminal possession of a weapon, he could have been sentenced to 25 years to life for those offenses, but he was somehow permitted to plead guilty to

attempted rape in November, 1977. In January, 1978, Supreme
Court Justice Pasquale E. DiVernieri sentenced Lynch to 1 to 10
years, refusing to grant the rapist youthful offender status. Though
16 years old, the severity of his crimes had influenced the
judge's decision.

Lynch was denied release when he came before the parole
board in early 1978, and denied again in November and December
of 1979, before finally being granted parole on August, 1982.
Paul Young, a spokesman for the New York State Parole Board,
said that Lynch was under psychiatric care, but had received
no treatment while in prison. Young stated that even if Lynch
had been denied parole when he was released, he would have
automatically been released in 18 months.

This recent, October, 1982 attack occurred at about 6:15
pm on Friday, October 1st, in a field off Madsen Ave. The female
victim had just exited a Staten Island Rapid Transit train at the
Richmond Valley station and was beginning her walk home, when
Lynch allegedly approached her. Threatening her with a knife, he
forced her into the field and raped her.

Lynch, now of 87-97 25th Ave, Brooklyn (where he was staying
with his father) was a former Mount Loretto resident. His mother
resided in South Shore. While we knew that he hadn't been the
only man committing rapes on Staten Island – as some attacks
continued while he was in custody, he was the prime suspect for a
number of other related assaults. It was certainly a relief to have
this guy off the streets once more.

Andrew Nielsen, 43, finished his shift at the Oakwood Sewage
Treatment Plant at midnight, December 3, 1982, and stopped
by a tavern for a drink. At just past 1:30am, police found him
unconscious and bleeding from the head on the tavern floor.

Almost a month after being admitted to the Staten Island
Hospital, Nielsen was still not coherent enough to give me an
accurate account of what had happened on the night of the attack
in Marion's Club Nostalgia, formerly known as Toddy's Bar. This
was a beachfront establishment at 67 Foxbeach Avenue, where the
victim was known to have occasionally stopped on his way home
from work. While the tavern had reportedly been crowded with

people, none of the bar's patrons or employees had been willing to come forward to furnish an account of what had happened. Though we questioned everyone we could locate, Lt. William Quinn of the Crimes Against Persons Squad stated the results.

"It's one of those situations where everybody was either in the bathroom or at the cigarette machine."

Nielsen, married and the father of a 17 year old son and 15 year old daughter, was still in the hospital for Christmas, unable to return to his home at 341 Corbin Avenue, Great Kills. He was sent to Staten Island Hospital where he was treated for his injuries. At month's end, he was removed from the critical list and taken off the Intensive Care Unit after he had regained consciousness. Unfortunately, Mr. Nielsen went back into a coma and died on Thursday, January 6, 1983 while at the hospital of two blows to his skull with a blunt instrument.

Harold Foner, Chairman of the Policemen's Benevolent Association Sports Foundation of New York City offered a $1000 reward for information leading to the arrest and conviction of the person or persons responsible, with a phone number listed for confidential disclosure.

Many friends of the victim joined Nielsen's widow in pleading for anyone to come forward immediately by making contact with the police. One friend, Ann Christensen, wrote a letter to the Staten Island Advance who published it. In it she stated: "We all know that something is terribly wrong when we allow this to happen and do nothing. You are guilty if you remain silent and allow the murderer(s) to walk free. You have a moral responsibility to speak. A man, Andrew Nielsen, was beaten. He later died. As a result, two children are fatherless, a woman is a widow, a good friend is lost, a co-worker is missed, elderly parents are told their only child is dead, a grieving mother dies and a community mourns the loss of a member" she wrote.

Despite these passionate pleas, Detective Fahey and I never heard from any of the many people in the bar that night, when a birthday party was in progress. Thus, we were unfortunately unable to solve this violent murder.

On Sunday, January 30, 1983 Robert Fahey and I did arrest a 24-year-old man in connection with a purse snatching earlier in the month. Brian Tyler, 24, of West Brighton was charged with two counts of robbery and one count of possession of a weapon.
On January 15 Tyler had allegedly robbed Evelyn Ventro, 24 of West Brighton at gunpoint at the corner of Wayne Terrace and Wayne Street, also West Brighton, demanding her pocketbook. Ms. Ventro surrendered her pocketbook, which had no money in it at the time of the incident.

After the robbery Ms. Ventro saw Tyler on the street and identified him, leading to his arrest.

Staten Island Advance

Vol. 97. No. 20,670   38 Pages 20 Cents   Copyright 1982 by Advance Publications Inc.   Staten Island, N.Y. Tuesday October 5, 1982   Home-delivered daily and Sunday. $1.25 a week

Man seized in South Shore rape

Probe connection to 2 other attacks

By LORI WEINRAUB
and LEONARD DREY

A 21-year-old Brooklyn man, released from prison about a month ago after serving five years for attempted rape, was arrested yesterday in connection with the rape of a 17-year-old Richmond Valley girl last Friday, police said.

Even as he was being arrested, however, another in a string of attacks on women in the Tottenville-Richmond Valley area took place. In yesterday's incident, which police stressed was apparently unrelated, a 14-year-old Tottenville girl fought off a knife-wielding man who approached her at the corner of Arthur Kill Road and Main Street.

The suspect in last Friday's rape, Patrick Lynch, of 87-97 25th Ave., Brooklyn, a former Mount Loretto resident, was arrested yesterday afternoon by Detectives Saverio DeMorato and Gary Rosen of the Crimes Against Persons Squad, and has been charged with rape, possession of a weapon and unlawful imprisonment.

Lynch was apprehended when he appeared for a meeting with his parole officer yesterday morning. He was released from the Elmira Correctional Facility on Aug. 27, where he had been held since September 1977 when he was convicted of a South Shore rape

that year.

Lynch was living with his father in Brooklyn at the time of his arrest. Authorities said his mother is a South Shore resident, but they would not say in which community she lived. Lynch was living at Mount Loretto when he was arrested in 1977.

According to police, last Friday's rape occurred about 6:15 p.m. in a field off Madsen Avenue. The victim had gotten off a Staten Island Rapid Transit train at the Richmond Valley station and was heading home when she was allegedly approached by Lynch. He apparently threatened her with a knife and forced her into the field, police said.

On Sept. 19, a 39-year-old woman was raped shortly after 3 p.m. at Camden Street and Page Avenue, also in Richmond Valley. And last Wednesday, a woman was confronted in the parking lot of the A & P in Tottenville. Descriptions of the man given in all three cases were similar, police said.

Lynch has not been charged in the other incidents, but Sgt. Arthur Carney of the persons squad said the investigation was continuing. "We're looking at the other incidents for connections," he said.

Carney said the 17-year-old

(See RAPE, Page A 7)

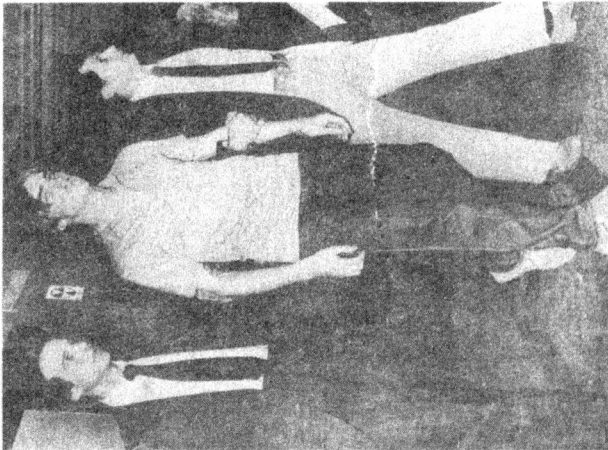

Rape suspect Patrick Lynch, 21, of Brooklyn, a former Pleasant Plains resident, arrives at the 122nd Precinct stationhouse, New Dorp, with Detectives Gary Rosen, left, and Saverio DeMorato.
S.I. Advance Photo by Tony Caranna

Rape

(From Page A 1)

rape victim identified Lynch as the man who raped her.

In yesterday's incident, the girl was grabbed around 7 a.m. by a man armed with a knife. She was dragged to the rear of 93 Main St., but she managed to escape by kicking the man in the groin when he was distracted by a neighbor emptying garbage.

The girl's description of her assailant, howevver, differed from descriptions provided by the other victims. The other women had identified their assailant as having blond hair, but the girl said she was attacked by a man with black hair.

Sgt. Patrick Bradley of the persons squad said there was "good and sufficient reason" to believe that yesterday's incident was unrelated to the others.

Lynch was arrested on Sept. 5, 1977, and charged in the rape of a 15-year-old Richmond Valley girl on Aug. 30 of that year. Lynch apparently threatened the girl with a razor and forced her into the woods about 300 feet west of Weiner Street on Richmond Valley Road, near the SIRT station, where she was raped.

He was also charged with the attempted rape and robbery of a Pleasant Plains woman on Aug. 15, 1977, near her home.

In November, Lynch was permitted to plead guilty to an attempted rape. He had originally been charged with sodomy, rape, attempted rape, attempted sodomy, two counts of sexual abuse, two counts of robbery and two counts of criminal possession of a weapon.

He could have been sentenced to 25 years to life for those offenses, said Paul Young, a spokesman for the New York State Parole Board.

In January, 1978, Supreme Court Justice Pasquale E. DiVernieri sentenced Lynch to one to 10 years in prison. He refused to grant youthful offender status to Lynch, even though he was 16 years old at the time.

Lynch was eligible for parole less than a year after he entered prison. Because he had been in jail since his arrest in September, he was credited with time already served and came before the parole board in early 1978, Young said.

But because of the seriousness of Lynch's offenses, his parole was denied, Young said. Lynch appeared before the board again in November 1979 and in December 1981, before he was finally granted parole in August. Young said that even if parole had been denied, Lynch would have automatically been released in 18 months.

Young said that Lynch was under psychiatric care, but received no treatment while in prison.

"I don't know if the judge was right or wrong in sentencing him to one to 10 years," Young said. "None of us have the answer."

Chapter Nineteen

When I was living at 6 Windham Loop in the New Springfield section of Staten Island, a man named Anthony Ercolano lived in the same condo complex as I, at #18.

When I regularly walked my dogs, I would often encounter some of my neighbors. While on one such dog walk I met Ercolano, who introduced me to his wife Marion, and I later met him on a number of occasions. During one of my conversations with Ercolano, I mentioned that I was a cop. He told me that he had a nephew who was a cop in Jersey City.

Though we never became friends, I did approach him regarding one of the cars he owned that was for sale. It was an older Fiat automobile, yellow in color, with a "for sale" sign in the car's window. The indicated price was $900. After I took the car for a test drive, I asked Ercolano if he could do any better. We agreed on $800, so I bought the Fiat. There was a large, blond man present at the time of the sale, but we weren't introduced and I didn't learn his name.

On the night of Wednesday, May 11, 1983 at about 9:10pm someone fired a single shotgun blast through the front door of Ercolano's home. Ercolano had heard someone knock and had come to answer the heavy steel door. When he looked through the door's peephole, he saw a man standing in the hallway, cradling a shotgun.

Ercolano quickly backed away from the door, as the man outside fired, narrowly missing him. A single shotgun pellet blew through the steel door, lodging in a china cabinet against the far wall. A deer pellet, about the size of a marble, is slightly larger than a .45 caliber slug and could easily cause a fatal wound.

Two witnesses saw the assailant walk away after firing the shotgun, and watched as he entered a black pickup truck. Both license plates on the truck were covered over with white cloth. The assailant drove away in the truck.

Bobby Fahey and I were performing a 4-1 tour of duty. While in the squad room, we were informed that there had been a shooting at 18 Windham Loop. "Did you hear that address?" asked Fahey. He knew that I lived in that condo, so the news was alarming. We immediately responded to the scene to investigate.

We learned that the shooting occurred at the home of Anthony Ercolano. During the investigation I interviewed Ercolano, looking for a motive for the shooting, and the identification of the assailant. Fortunately, Mrs. Ercolano wasn't home at the time, a genuine relief for Anthony.

As to the shotgun shooter, Ercolano told me, "You've seen the guy. He was the one who was with me when you came to buy the car." He gave me the name of the shooter, a guy referred to as "Whitey", a gambler who lived in Elizabeth, New Jersey.

Ercolano did tell me he was involved in bookmaking in New Jersey, so I then ran a check with BCI to ascertain if there were any Wants or Warrants. If he was wanted in New York on any charges, I didn't want to be in the uncomfortable position of having to arrest a neighbor: I'd have had the case reassigned to a different detective. I was relieved to learn that he was clean in New York.

The next day duty, Detective Fahey and I went over to the Elizabeth, New Jersey Police Dept, and conferred with their detectives. They were familiar with both Ercolano and the assailant. They then shared information about Anthony Ercolano and his brother Enrico, from as early as 1976, when the Elizabeth Police Department was investigating a gambling activity conspiracy.

The Elizabeth, New Jersey Detectives, who knew both the assailant and where he resided, soon made the arrest. After they collared him in Jersey he was taken to the Union County Jail. When we were notified of his arrest there, we secured an arrest warrant for New York. Having learned that the prisoner was willing to waive extradition, Fahey and I drove to the Union County Jail to pick him up and bring him back to Staten Island for arrest processing and arraignment. The subject was charged with attempted murder and possession of a weapon. At arraignment at Richmond County Criminal Court, the defendant was remanded.

The subject was later indicted by the Richmond County Grand Jury. "Whitey" decided that he wanted to go to trial. At the trial, the defendant insinuated that I had been involved with Ercolano, who he alleged had offered to give me a special price on the Fiat. The evidence against the defendant was sufficient for a conviction, and he was sentenced to time in prison.

Chapter Twenty

Detective Michael Wilk and I were assigned to the case of a 23-year-old West Brighton man who was shot on the left side of his chest.

The victim, Cyril Dixon, had been taken to St. Vincent's Medical Center after the shooting by one of his brothers. The incident took place in front of 139 Braybrant St. in Mariner's Harbor at 12:30am. There had reportedly been only one shot fired, according to witnesses. Later that morning Dixon was listed in stable condition.

Dixon told Wilk and me that he knew the shooter "slightly" and didn't know why he was shot. He reportedly was wounded while standing next to his cousin, who'd been talking to the gunman on the street. Dixon stated that he and his cousin had been there for "only a few minutes" when the shooting occurred. According to him, about 10 people witnessed the crime.

We surveyed the crime scene that morning, interviewing some of the witnesses. Though we were unable to immediately track down Dixon's cousin, we expected to reach him later that day.

Police who had fanned out throughout the North Shore and ferry terminal areas, briefly believed that they'd nabbed the suspect. "We picked up someone with a similar description, but it was not the shooter," said Sgt. Eugene Martinez of the Staten Island Crimes Against Persons Squad. When witnesses at the hospital stated that the man we picked up was not the suspect, he was released.

Witnesses did report that the gunman used a small automatic handgun, and was seen running toward South Avenue after shooting Dixon. We believed that the gunman, known as "Vinny" and "Uptown Vinny", lived in Manhattan. His description: about 20-years-old, 5' 10" tall, 165 pounds, with brown hair and eyes. At the time of the crime he was reportedly wearing a shiny black jacket, a gray, hooded sweatshirt, blue jeans and a black baseball hat.

On October 11, 1983 there was a home robbery in Grant City, during which jewelry and a car were stolen. This was another case which I investigated.

A woman named America Samaritano, who lived at the home, had advertised a car that she owned which was for sale. That afternoon she was home with two friends: Susan Carucci of Bulls Head, and Catherine Imperatore of Mariners Harbor. At 1:30 pm a man – described as being in his mid-twenties, went to her home, ostensibly to purchase the car. After entering her house the man drew a gun and took the women to a bedroom, where he handcuffed Mrs. Samaritano and tied up Mrs. Carucci and Mrs. Imperatore.

According to the complaint filed with the police, the man then took two diamond rings, valued at a total of $25,000, a gold pendant, valued at $1,000, and several credit cards from Mrs. Samaritano. He also took two diamond rings, valued at a total of $16,500 and $500 in cash from Mrs. Carucci.

The man then left in Mrs. Samaritano's car, a tan 1982 Oldsmobile. After the women got free, Mrs. Samaritano went to a neighbor's home, from where she called the police.

Two bandits, wielding guns, handcuffed a Willowbrook jewelry salesman on February 14, 1984. They robbed him of a briefcase filled with expensive merchandise.

According to the victim, Joseph Bittar, 46, the unidentified men assaulted him outside 23 Saybrook St., Willowbrook at about 9 am, as he was preparing to get into his car. Bittar reported that one of the men put a gun to his head and ordered him to turn over his merchandise. The robbers then handcuffed the victim.

Assigned to investigate the case, I sought to determine how the robbers knew that Bittar would be in possession of the jewelry. The value of the stolen jewelry was undetermined. Sergeant Arthur Carney of the Crimes Against Persons Squad again asked for community assistance, listing a phone number to call with any information on the incident.

Epilogue

As I was advised to notify the PD of my condition, I went to see the PD Surgeon and informed him of the findings. The department required you to report to a Police Surgeon if you were going to be out for more than two days. The Police Surgeon for Staten Island was Dr. Lagmey, who worked out of Seaview Hospital. I had seen him several times, and he cleared me so I could return to duty.

Dr. Lagmey conferred with my pulmonologist and then contacted Lt. Quinn, my squad commander. Dr. Lagmey told Lt. Quinn to place me on light-duty. The PD also had some of the top doctors in New York City, titled Honorary Surgeons, who assisted officers with serious medical conditions. The Medical Unit made an appointment for me to see Dr. Murray Rogers on 5th Ave. in Manhattan for an examination. He concurred with my doctor's diagnosis. Dr. Rogers stated that because this disease is incurable I would never be able to return to full duty. He further stated that he was going to recommend to the Medical Board that a Disability Retirement be granted. He also suggested that I move to a warm climate.

I returned to the squad and informed Lt. Quinn and Sgt. Bradley of Dr. Roger's retirement recommendation. It would now be a matter of months before I would get called to go before the Medical Board. Usually, if a member of the department was never going to return to full duty, he or she would be assigned to the Restricted Duty Unit located at the Police Academy in Manhattan, while waiting to be surveyed out of the department. In my case, it meant that I would lose my 7% Night Differential and any overtime I accumulated. Lt. Quinn made some phone calls on my behalf. He was able to keep me in the squad, continue with my team's duty chart (Night Differential) and allow me to accumulate more overtime, which permitted me to reach a Detective's one hundred hour yearly cash cap. Though I couldn't catch cases or make arrests, I was able to assist other team members with their investigations, including interviews and canvasses.

In March of 85, I went before the Medical Board and was approved for a disability retirement. I began to use whatever vacation time I had coming along with my terminal leave days. My official date of retirement was April 29, 1985.

During my nearly 17 years with the department I accumulated the following medals:

- 1 Commendation
- 8 Meritorious Police Duty
- 6 Excellent Police Duty
- 1 Proclamation from the Staten Island Borough President designating April 29th as Gary Rosen Day
- 1 Citation from the New York City Council thanking me for my service to the people of the City of New York

Following my approval by the Medical Board, I flew down to Florida and contracted to have a house built in the City of Coral Springs. There were two reasons for moving to this particular city. One reason was that this is where my father now lived with his wife and two sons. The other was that I learned that the Coral Springs school system was one of only two school systems in the State of Florida that did not bus their students out of their city. Since my daughter Jodi would be going into first grade, it was very important to me to get her into a good school system that was close to home. Coral Springs was an upper income city, and because of their school policy, the average home cost at least $25,000 more than for the same house in one of the surrounding cities.

In June of 1985 my wife, daughter and I moved to our new home in Florida. My Dad informed me of a club that was made up strictly of retired New York City Police Officers. The club was called the 10-13 Club of Broward County. I joined the club and learned that 10-13 Clubs were being developed throughout the State of Florida. The clubs were originally formed for socialization. I attended monthly meetings where I met other former cops that I had worked with, and made friends with others that I hadn't known from the job. The Broward Club at this time was the largest of all the clubs in Florida, with approximately 900 members. Many of these members were snowbirds. Also, at this time I rekindled my friendship with Bill Creelman who was also a member of the Club, and now a Detective with the City of Margate Police Department.

New York City was again going through a financial crisis, and there was talk that the city was looking to diminish benefits like medical coverage for retirees. Even though we were still members of the various NYPD Unions, under the New York State Taylor Law, the unions were not allowed to represent their retirees. At this point, all the 10-13 Clubs became political. 10-13 Clubs began to emerge throughout New York City and the surrounding counties. Clubs were also beginning to form in other states. Because of the large amount of retirees belonging to these clubs, we were able to retain our benefits and were even able to get us an annual Cost of Living Adjustment to our pensions.

There is an old saying: "Once a New York City Cop, always a New York City Cop", even after retirement. We soon discovered that we cops from NYC had a unique brotherhood that looked out for one another, while police officers in Florida had no such loyalty to each other. It was not uncommon for one cop in Florida to give another cop a ticket, even if both worked for the same city. In New York, professional courtesy was always given to another officer and his family. If you gave a ticket to another cop in New York, chances were your locker would be thrown out of the third floor locker room window.

In 1994 my daughter was set to go into high school. I decided to sell my home and move up to Boca Raton, which was in Palm Beach County. I dropped out of the Broward County 10-13 Club and joined the Palm Beach County 10-13 Club. This club was a smaller chapter where I again met many members I'd known while on the job, and where I again made new friends. Jerimiah O'Connor, my former captain in narcotics, was also a Palm Beach County member. We renewed our friendship, and engaged in some social activities. While I had been a member of both clubs, I never had any aspirations to get politically involved by becoming a board member.

In 1996 I bought myself a Harley Davidson Heritage Soft
Tail motorcycle. By the time I was done customizing this bike,
I was into it for some serious money. It looked like something
out of the 1950s with lots of chrome, wide whitewall tires and
leather saddle bags. The only thing missing was a kick starter,
which Harley had done away with for an electric starter. The bike
brought back some good and bad memories. As I mentioned in
the beginning of this book, I spent much time with my father in
Coney Island. One Friday night when I was about 6 or 7, my father
took me to Nathan's to get something to eat. In front of Nathan's
along Surf Ave., there were about 20 tripped out Harleys parked.
All the owners of the bikes were just hanging out, wearing black
motorcycle jackets, black T shirts and blue jeans with black boots
– real tough looking guys. I had told my father, "When I grow up
I want to be one of them." Till this day, I can still feel the crack
on my face that my father gave me. My favorite movie was the
"Wild One" starring Marlon Brando. One bad memory was of the
motorcycle accident that I had in 1969.

Although I had many cop friends, it was difficult for me to become close friends with any civilians. I found that I had nothing in common with them. In 1985 when I moved to Florida and I needed a mortgage for my new home, I met David Goldstein who had his own mortgage company. Instantly, I sensed that an immediate bond had been established.

I learned that David was an accomplished musician and a philanthropist, who donated serious money to various charities and causes. He came from an affluent family, and his wife Hope was a high powered real estate broker. As a banker, he was unorthodox in his appearance, with long silver hair, sometimes worn in a pony tail. An impressive dresser, David wore clothing quite unlike his contemporaries in this conservative field. Maybe it was his long hair, or the fact that we were both from Brooklyn, that a mutual respect and a long-lasting friendship developed. David relished the fact that I was a NYPD Detective and that I had an uncanny sense of being street wise. In his heart, he believed that everyone was good. Unfortunately this belief allowed some people to try to take advantage of his good nature. He dabbled in many businesses and ventures, some that made him a lot of money, and some that turned out to be scams. Because of his generosity, there were those who considered him an easy mark.

If I had any problems, David was always there to offer assistance. I considered him a gift from God. I then made it my responsibility to cover his back and keep him from being harmed. David had overcome a life threatening illness, from which he was lucky to survive. I would often sit in on meetings when pitches were made to David for him to personally finance new construction sites, developments and other so-called business opportunities. David knew my ability to read people, and trusted my instincts when I sometimes told him I suspected nefarious motives, and suggested that he pass on the deal presented to him. Unfortunately, his wife Hope became ill with a terminal disease which required numerous hospitalizations. David spared no expense for Hope's medical treatments, which included the best private room in the Boca Raton hospital. Even after exhausting Hope's medical coverage, and facing the fact that there was no cure, David continued to pay out of pocket for her treatments and hospital stays, until she passed. After being married for many years David looked like a lost soul.

As time went on, David met a widow named Maxine, a fine lady who was equally beautiful on both the inside and the outside. She was a dentist and owned her own practice in Boca Raton. As their relationship blossomed, David sold his home and moved in with Maxine. I was thrilled for both of them. David and Maxine came up to Palm Coast to attend my daughter's wedding. David, being a Public Notary, officiated at the wedding. I speak with David on a weekly basis.

When my daughter graduated from Boca Raton High School she decided to go to college. At this point in her life, she no idea of what she wanted for a career.

The real estate business was very hot and people became brokers by the dozens. Most were not full time and only looked to get listings, hoping for another broker to get a buyer for their listing. David Goldstein was now working for CTX Mortgage, which was a division of Centex Homes. I brought Jodi up to David's office to meet him. David had something framed on the wall behind his desk. Jodi asked David what it was, so David took it off the wall to show her more closely. It was a picture of a $28,000 commission check for a mortgage that David had earned. Jodi was very impressed and stated that this is what she would like to do. David gave her the name of a school that taught real estate and mortgage brokering, informing her that she would have to attend such a school in order to get licensed by the State.

I brought my daughter over to the school she needed to attend. When we walked in together, I immediately saw that my daughter was intimidated by the people that were there to register. They were all in their 40s, 50s and 60s. She looked at me and said: "I don't know, Dad." At this point in my life, I was quite content, retired and riding my Harley. To put her at ease, I told her that I would take the course with her. We both signed up that day. The course lasted several months, and upon completion we took the State Mortgage Broker's Exam at the same time. We both passed the exam and Jodi, at 20 years of age, became the youngest mortgage broker in the State of Florida. Jodi was hired with a mortgage company that handled people with C and D paper, which was bad credit.

About a year and a half went by when Jodi told me she was not happy with the company she was with. She felt bad for many of her clients who were charged high rates of interest for their mortgages, including additional points and other fees. She also felt that many of the applications submitted were not truthful, especially when it came to verification of income and employment. I called David Goldstein and set up an appointment for me and Jodi to meet with him.

The following week we met at David's office and Jodi expressed her concerns with him. David was now the Production Manager for CTX. He told Jodi that CTX didn't hire mortgage brokers who had less than 10 years' experience. However, he would set Jodi up with the company's Vice President for an interview. He was really going out on the limb for her. Several days later, Jodi was interviewed by the Vice President who asked Jodi, "What percent of loan applications do you close?" Jodi told him that all of her loans closed. He asked how could that be. She told him that if applicants couldn't meet the qualifications needed to get the mortgage, she would be up front with them and not have them put themselves in a position to have to lie, which would be criminal. She further stated that she processed her own loans.

He asked her, "Doesn't the company you work for have processors?"

She said, "Yes, but I wanted my loans to close."

The processor was the one to take all the information from the broker and prepare a package to go to underwriting. If required items were missing or the forms submitted were incorrect, the underwriter would reject the loan. Because Jodi had been doing this herself, she knew her loans would close. The VP was so impressed with Jodi's integrity and work ethic that he waived the hiring rule and hired her.

I went back to riding my Harley and socializing with my cop friends. The 10-13 clubs had many functions during the course of the year. This included an annual picnic and dinner dance. Attending masses and funerals became more frequent for me, as our members continued to age.

Gary Rosen
911 Police Commemorative Harley Davidson Electra Glide
2003

After 9/11, Harley Davidson produced two commemorative motorcycles. Both were Electra Glides, with one produced in all red for firefighters and one in all blue for police officers. In order to purchase either one, you had to be a firefighter or police officer {active or retired}. Agency ID had to be produced at the time of sale. In 2003, I purchased the Electra Glide in Blue. Unlike my Soft Tail, the Electra Glide was rubber mounted which gave you a smooth ride – like driving a Lincoln Town Car. I would pop in a CD and drive for hours. I ordered a custom license plate from the State. NYPD749. The cop was still in me.

In July of 2005, CTX offered my daughter Jodi a promotion which would require her to relocate. Centex Homes was one of the nation's largest builders. The company was constructing many high-end developments in the City of Palm Coast, which was located in Flagler County, Florida. Jodi had been interviewed by the President who was in charge of this area, and she offered her the position of Exclusive Mortgage Broker for these developments. Jodi accepted the offer and was scheduled to start her new assignment in September.

The real estate market in Boca Raton was very hot. My wife Christine and I decided that we would sell our home and move with Jodi, our only child. Since I was retired, there was nothing holding me back from moving. Rather than having Jodi move to a place where she knew no one, I told her we would be selling our home and we would make the move with her. Jodi was thrilled and I was happy that our family would still be together. Another plus for me was the fact that I was now moving into bike country. Palm Coast was right above Daytona Beach which had Bike Week and Biketoberfest which I attended on an annual basis.

I placed our home up for sale and was able to sell it within two weeks for top dollar. A late August closing date was set. We made several trips up to Palm Coast and hooked up with a Realtor®. New inventory was then in short supply. With my closing date coming up fast, I had to settle on purchasing a new home that was not in a gated community and in a sub division I didn't care for. The Realtor® informed me that there were many retired NYPD cops living in Palm Coast and that there was also a 10-13 Club in the area.

In October, I joined the Northeast Florida 10-13 Club and was warmly greeted by the Club President Eddie Woods, who was a retired sergeant. The meeting took place in Ormond Beach. Eddie asked me to stand, and he introduced me to the membership. I gave a short biography of myself and my time with the NYPD. As I was speaking, I looked around and did not see anyone that I knew from the job. I then sat down and a member sitting next to me turned to me.

"Gary! How have you been?"

I looked at him in bewilderment.

He then said, "Gary, I'm Mike Magana."

A bell went off in my head. Mike had been one of my backup guys when I worked in narcotics. I had not seen Mike since the early 70's. Time had really taken a toll on our appearances. We rekindled our friendship until Mike passed away in 2020. I also learned that Joe Zachary, who'd been another one of my backup men and was also a member of the club, had died too in 2019.

When I attended the November meeting a huge argument erupted, with many of the older members cursing and throwing personal insults at Eddie Woods. This was the result of Eddie's having our club become a member of one of two National 10-13 Organizations. It seemed that the older members wanted to keep our club isolated, by not joining either National Organization until there was unity between both. There had been a previous vote with regard to this matter. Eddie and the current board believed it was in the club's best interest to become a member of one of the Nationals. New York City always seemed to be in a financial crisis and was looking to take benefits away from retirees. As a retiree you still remained a member of your union, whether it was the PBA (Patrolman), DEA (Detectives), SBA (Sergeants), LBA (Lieutenants), or CEA (Captains). As a member of your union, you would receive a prescription drug plan, dental plan, optical plan and any other benefits that your union provided. The City gave each union funds to provide these services. However, the New York State Taylor Law prohibited the unions from representing retired members. All the other 10-13 Clubs belonged to either one of the Nationals. Both Nationals operated differently, but both had the same goal, which was to protect the retirees' benefits. There was strength in numbers. At this time, in Florida alone there were 15,000 NYPD retirees. Eddie took a bad beating that night but stood by his conviction that he had done the right thing. At the end of the meeting I spoke with Eddie and I told him that I understood what he was doing and offered him my allegiance. Eddie explained that the older members started the club as the Volusia County 10-13 Club and incorporated the club in 1982. Realizing that there were many more cops that lived in Palm Coast, Flagler County and Saint Johns County, the club's name changed to the Northeast Florida 10-13 Club.

My wife and I attended the annual Christmas Dinner Dance where I met more members that I knew, and became friends with many more, like Jack Murray and John Briganti, who to this day I consider to be some of my closest friends.

After about 6 months of living in Palm Coast, my daughter Jodi fell in love with a young gentleman named Larry, who she'd been dating. Larry's family was also from Brooklyn. Larry and his parents were in the food business and eventually opened up one of the most successful restaurants in Palm Coast. Jodi and Larry became engaged and about a year later they married. They gave us two grandchildren: both a girl and a boy!

In April of 2006, I attended the club's annual picnic which was run by Jack Murray, who had the assistance of other club members. Approximately 200 members with their families and friends attended this function. Jack and his crew prepared all the food on-site, which included various meats, salads, and pasta dishes, along with beer, wine and soda beverages. I would soon learn in the coming years that this was the most attended get together of the year – a very enjoyable event. Christine and I remained until the end of the picnic. The only other person who was still there was the Club's Vice President, Milt Williams, who began collecting all the trash left behind. We pitched in, helping Milt clean up. Milt was a retired sergeant who had a son that was also a cop with the NYPD. Milt's son David had taken an early vested retirement and was now was a motorcycle cop with the Flagler County Sheriff's Office. I asked Milt what his desire was with the club. Milt told me that he wanted to be the first black president of the club, but felt that because he was getting up in the years he would be unable to serve a full term as president. I never forgot what he'd said.

While out for lunch with a group of members and our spouses, Jack Murray, who was a widower, attended the luncheon with his girlfriend Maria, a beautiful young lady. At this occasion, Jack and Maria stated that they were getting married and invited some of us to their wedding, to take place in September of 2006. Christine and I did attend the wedding which was like a Hollywood Production! Maria presented as one of the classiest ladies you could ever meet. Jack was very handsome, and coupled with Maria's beauty, I truly found them be the best looking couple in the club.

John Briganti and his wife Anita invited Christine and me over to their house for a barbecue, along with several other club members. Anita and John had been married for many years. Sadly, a short time after this gathering Anita passed away and John became a lost soul. When I was with John I could see an emptiness in his eyes and I wondered if he was ever going to recover from his loss.

In early 2007, Marty Fitzgerald, the club's Sgt. At Arms, got into a bicycle accident and was seriously hurt. Eddie Woods asked me to take over Marty's position and become a club board member. I told Eddie I was not into politics, but Eddie told me that he needed me. As a courtesy, before accepting this position I called Marty and asked him if he was okay with this arrangement. Marty gave me his blessing. Once coming onto the board, I became very close with Eddie. He then became my mentor.

In both 2007 and 2008 Eddie invited me to attend our National's yearly convention in upstate New York. Eddie, being the president, was comped by the club for any expense with regard to the convention. This included airfare, hotel, car rental and a $50 per diem cash award. Eddie knew that it would cost me a considerable amount of money if I was going to attend, so he offered to split his stipend with me so I could attend. I later returned this favor to Eddie when I became president. At the convention, Eddie introduced me to all the presidents of the other chapters. I knew the national president, Tony Perrone, from working on Staten Island. Also in attendance was Harry Morse, whom I'd met when coming on the job, and had also worked on Staten Island. Harry's dad had been on the job at the same time as my father. One of the highlights for me at the convention was seeing my friend John Briganti, who was keeping company with the new love of his life. Prior to the convention, John had been asked to give a ride to one of our meetings to a lovely lady named Trudy LaForgia. Trudy was a widow and a retired NYPD 2 Star Assistant Chief. I was thrilled for John! It was a match made in heaven.

These warm, personal stories served as supportive memories of the camaraderie we'd developed in our careers on the job in New York City.

On the way home from the 2008 convention, Eddie said he was going to be stepping down from being president. He wanted to know if I would be interested in running for the position. I was honest with him, and told him I didn't think I could fill his shoes. He eased my concern by stating that he would always be there to assist me. Then it hit me – I recalled my conversation with VP Milt Williams. Eddie told me that he had spoken with Milt and Milt wasn't up to it. I suggested to Eddie to let Milt take over the first three months of 2009 as president, and that I would then take over. By doing this I knew Milt's wish of being the first black president of the club would come true. Eddie then agreed to step down at the end of September so Milt could become president for the months of October, November and December, 2008. I told Eddie if this was okay with Milt, I would gladly become president in 2009.

During Eddie's tenure as president, the club grew tremendously. The Central Florida 10-13 Club, which took in the City of Orlando and the surrounding areas, merged into our club. The Villages, located in north central Florida, was brought into our club. Eddie had been cultivating this group to eventually become their own chapter. We were now the largest geographical club within the state of Florida, covering from Orlando to north central Florida, Ocala, Jacksonville, the Georgia border, St. Johns County, Flagler County, Volusia County and Seminole County. Eddie served as president from 2005-2008, and later became president again for 2012 and 2013. He was the club's longest serving president. In my opinion, he was the best president that the club ever had.

When I became president in 2009, my old friend Bill Creelman, who was now residing in Port St. Lucie, joined our club. Stu Weisbaum, another 67th Pct cop who resided in Ocala, also joined the club. Stu had left the 67 before I was assigned to the squad there. I had met Stu through Bill, when we were all members of the Broward 10-13 Club. The first thing I did as president was to heed Eddie Woods' suggestion to appoint advisors to assist me. These appointments included Eddie, Jack Murray, John Briganti, who'd joined the board as the club's Sergeant-at-Arms, and Al McEvoy, the former Police Commissioner of the Yonkers, New York Police Department. Al also served as the club's Chaplain. Milt Williams remained on the board as my VP, and Augie Lucente remained as Treasurer. When Milt decided to step down as VP on the recommendation of John Briganti, I appointed Joe Phillips to be my VP.

Another great asset to the club was Vic Nevins ,who served as a Trustee and the club's Parliamentarian. Although Vic had no political aspirations, he has served the club as a Trustee for more than 20 years. Vic knew the club by-laws inside out, so I always had him sit to the left of me on the dais (a raised platform at the front of the hall). If a procedural problem popped up, Vic would whisper in my ear how I should resolve the issue. I relied on his knowledge whenever I found myself in a tough situation.

Being a member of the PBA, Vic asked the union if it was possible to have PBA cards with our club's name on it. Because of his efforts, we became the first 10-13 Club to have its name printed on the PBA cards. At meetings, he would update the membership on any changes with regard to HR218 and inform the members when the next qualification shoot would take place. Although we never socialized outside of the club, I consider him a good friend.

A new Federal Law (HR218) was passed by then-President George Bush which would allow retired police officers to carry a concealed firearm anywhere in the country. Each state would set up its own qualifications for the issuance of this permit. The State of Florida required you to shoot once a year, showing your proficiency to qualify for this permit. These qualification shoots were conducted by the Sheriff's Office in each county. In Flagler County, the cost for taking this course was $75. Thanks to member Jack Lincks, I was introduced to Don Fleming, the Sheriff of Flagler County, and his Chief Deputy, Rick Look, and we all had lunch together. The Sheriff had been the former Chief of a small police department in New Jersey and had some cousins that were with the NYPD. I explained to Don that our club had many older members on a fixed income and that the $75 charge would be a hardship for them. Don agreed not to charge any of our members. A free qualification course was also offered by the Volusia County

Sheriff Ben Johnson. As a result of this new law, our membership began to swell. We now had over 400 members, making us the second largest club in the state of Florida.

As president, having a great board of directors and awesome advisors behind me, I was able to bring some fresh ideas into the club. While Eddie Woods was president, he had Mike Chitwood, the Chief of the Daytona Beach Police Department, attend one of our meetings as a guest speaker. Mike was a retired Philadelphia PD lieutenant before taking the job as chief with Daytona. Our club adopted the Daytona Beach PD, and on a annual basis would present an Officer of the Year Award to a deserving officer picked by Mike.

Milt Williams and John Briganti continued to run the annual baseball game at the Jackie Robinson Stadium. Jack Murray and his crew continued the annual club picnic. The annual Christmas Dinner Dance also remained scheduled. As a large percentage of our membership was made up of veterans, we established a Veteran's Day Luncheon on an annual basis. This included the Volusia County Sheriff's Office Ceremonial Unit who presented the Colours, along with a Pipes and Drum Band. Those veterans who attended the luncheon received a certificate of appreciation for their service. I appointed Roy Peron (also deceased - from coronavirus in 2020), who was one of our members and had survived throat cancer, as Chairman of the Cancer Support Group. A Scholarship Committee was formed and I appointed Al McEvoy as Chairman. I was also able to get our National organization to designate one of their $1000 scholarships to be named the *Patrolman Philip Cardillo Scholarship*.

The Villages at that time had 60 of our members residing within their town. We assisted them in becoming their own chapter. Our National President, Tony Perrone, presented them with seed money to get started. Eddie Woods continued doing the club's monthly newsletter, which was the best in the country. Eddie would send it out to all of the 10-13 Clubs regardless of which National they belonged to. Eddie also continued as our Pension Rep., with the responsibility of assisting widows of our departed members with all their needed notifications, and presenting them with a $250

Club Death Benefit check. We were the only club that provided this benefit.

Part of the job of being president was to attend funerals and masses for members and their spouses, as well as for any other immediate member of their family. I had grown very close to Eddie Woods and his wife Linda, who had a son named Tommy, residing with his parents. When visiting Eddie at his home, I would often spend time talking with Tommy. He was one of the most gentle and kind persons I'd ever met. One day I received a telephone call from Eddie that Tommy had passed away in their home. With a heavy heart, I attended the funeral. Though many years have passed, I have called Eddie every May 1st – the day that Tommy died, to let Eddie know that I was thinking of his son.

On July 13, 2009 I received a telephone call at home from a Lt. John McGovern of the NYPD Internals Affairs Unit. Lt. McGovern stated that the Police Commissioner at this time, Raymond Kelly, had ordered him to make contact with all the 10-13 Clubs to have them cease and desist using the NYPD shield and patch on our letterheads, club shirts, hats and license plates. Our club was the first one that he'd contacted. He threatened to sue me for Federal Trademark infringement, with the possibility of being arrested under the New York Administrative Code. I told him to "Come and get me." At this point I was so pissed off, I told John that he and Ray Kelly could go fuck themselves. The next call he made was to Richard Stone, president of the Arizona 10-13 Club, who also cursed him out.

In 1972, police officers from the 28th Pct. in Harlem responded to a 10-13 call at a Mosque headed by Louis Farrakhan. Four officers entered the front doors of the mosque and became trapped inside by a group of black Muslims. The officers were beaten and the gun belonging to Patrolman Philip Cardillo was taken from him – he was shot with his own gun. Rudy Andre, who is one of our members, responded to the scene but was unable to enter, discovering that the doors had been locked. Rudy broke one of the glass windows on the door and began shooting his gun into the mosque. When other units arrived, they forced their way into the mosque.

Cardillo died several days later from his gunshot wounds. Because of Rudy's actions, the other three officers were saved. Cardillo's murder was assigned to Detective Randy Jurgensen of the 28 Detective Squad to investigate. The city and police officials were under much political pressure, because the incident took place in a so-called House of Worship. The Mayor and Police Commissioner did not attend Cardillo's funeral. This was the largest police funeral, with over 5,000 officers attending. Due to my working undercover at the time, I was unable to attend the funeral. Randy Jurgensen constantly found roadblocks thrown before him during his investigation, which he detailed in a book that he wrote called Circle of Six.

For many years, the Cardillo murder reverberated throughout the department. Attempts to get the street that the 28th Pct. was on to be named after Cardillo failed. Timmy Motto, a former 28th Pct. Member, kept the Cardillo name alive. "Remember Cardillo" became the slogan. The PBA, FOP and 10-13 Clubs kept trying to rename the street, but to no avail. Todd Cardillo, the son of Phil, was only one year old when his father was killed and never had the opportunity to know his dad. Todd lived in Palm Coast and Eddie Woods, while president, brought him into the 10-13 club as an Honorary Member.

When I became president, I took my DEA union's motto *We Take Care of Our Own*, and had it placed on the top of our newsletter. I told Dennis Lynch, a cousin of Todd Cardillo, that I would try my best to make sure that Phil Cardillo was never forgotten. While president, I read that two black NYPD Detectives were shot and killed during a gun buy. This murder took place at Graves End Bay where years before I had made a drug purchase with Steve Spinelli. Shortly after the shootings, I read that the department was going to name two new police boats after each of the detectives killed. I called my Treasurer, Augie Lucente, who had been a Sergeant in the Harbor Unit. I asked Augie to contact his former unit, to find out if the city was purchasing any more police boats. Augie informed me that five new boats were to be coming in, and that the first boat, was to be the biggest and most expensive.

He suggested that I contact the Police Reserve, a group of high-powered business owners in NYC. They loved cops and had assisted families of cops killed in the line of duty. They'd provided financial aid and scholarships to these families. I called Mitch Levy, the president of the Police Reserve, and introduced myself to him. Discussing the Cardillo case, Mitch said that he knew all about it. I told him about the boats coming in, and about my idea of having the first boat named after Cardillo. Mitch said he would speak to Commissioner Bratton about my request. Several weeks later, when I got a call at home from the Commissioner, I thought someone was playing a joke on me. Not so. Bratton was well aware of the Cardillo case and the injustice that was done to Phil. Bratton then told me that the next boat would be named after Cardillo. Several months later a ceremony was held, and the police boat promised was christened the *Patrolman Philip Cardillo*. I was invited to attend, but was unable to travel because of a medical problem that I was experiencing. To me, this was the greatest accomplishment I had accomplished as president.

I served as the club's president in 2009, 2010, 2011, 2014 and 2015. I am currently a club trustee and Liaison to the National. The club threw me a surprise dinner to honor me, and I was presented with a most beautiful plaque which contained a full size Patrolman's Shield #10-13 and a full size gold Detective's Shield #749. I had found gold again. I only wished that my father had still been alive, so that he could have seen me receive this great honor.

During the course of my career and club membership, it was an honor to belong to the greatest fraternity in the world. I made many friends, some who have already departed, but the ones listed below, who shared with me good and bad times together, have always been there for one another. I consider them the Best of the Best. They are: Bill Creelman, Bobby Fahey, David Goldstein, Eddie Woods, Jack Murray and John Briganti. I salute you all.

Honorable Mention

As I'd previously mentioned, I first met Stu Weisbaum at a Broward County 10-13 meeting. Stu had retired in February of 1974 from the 67th Pct., 9 months before I was assigned to the 67 Squad. Bill Creelman had introduced me to Stu at the meeting and we became good friends. In 1992 Stu moved from south Florida to the Ocala area. As earlier noted, when I became President of the Northeast Florida 10-13 Club, both Stu and Bill became members.

Stu had been camping in Riverton, Connecticut, located in the northwest part of the state on September 11, 2001. On the 14th of September, Stu drove down to New York City to aid in the rescue operations at the World Trade Center. Upon arriving in New York, Stu identified himself as a retired NYPD officer. He was told to report to the Jacob Javits Center to get logged in. Stu had been retired from the job for 27 years, yet volunteered to render assistance. This really amazed me and touched my heart.

On September 15th, Stu reported to the pit and was assigned to the Bucket Brigade. Stu was issued boots, gloves, a hard hat and safety goggles. The air was foul from the clouds of smoke. The smell of death was everywhere. Stu performed 20 hours of duty, each day, through September 21st. He then left New York, to return home to Ocala, Florida.

Upon returning home, Stu started having respiratory problems along with nose bleeds. As time went on, Stu found his overall health in steady decline. Eventually, in January of 2009, he signed up with the World Trade Center Health Program. Stu was diagnosed with numerous medical conditions which were directly related to his exposure to toxins at the World Trade Center. As his condition deteriorated on a daily basis, he experienced severe headaches, suffered a chronic cough, nose bleeds and stomach pains. His extreme respiratory problems required him to use a CPAP Machine. He needed be on oxygen every night, and his health has continued to deteriorate. I gladly maintain contact with my dear friend Stu on a weekly basis.

Stu was one of many thousands of active and retired cops who volunteered to work at the World Trade Center. A significant number of them developed various types of cancers and other life-threatening diseases, and many have died because of their exposure to all the toxins in the air and on the ground. I salute them all.

Stu has a daughter who is a police officer with the U.S. Park Police in Washington, D.C.

~

As a New York City Cop working the streets, all you ever see is evil. Year after year, you become more cynical, suspicious and calloused. It not only takes a toll on you, but oftentimes you don't realize what price your family has to pay, as you gradually become another person that they do not know.

Those sacrifices aside, my career in the New York City Police Department was immeasurably rewarding. I am proud of my honest efforts and successes, and those of my brothers and sisters in blue, to protect and serve the people of New York.

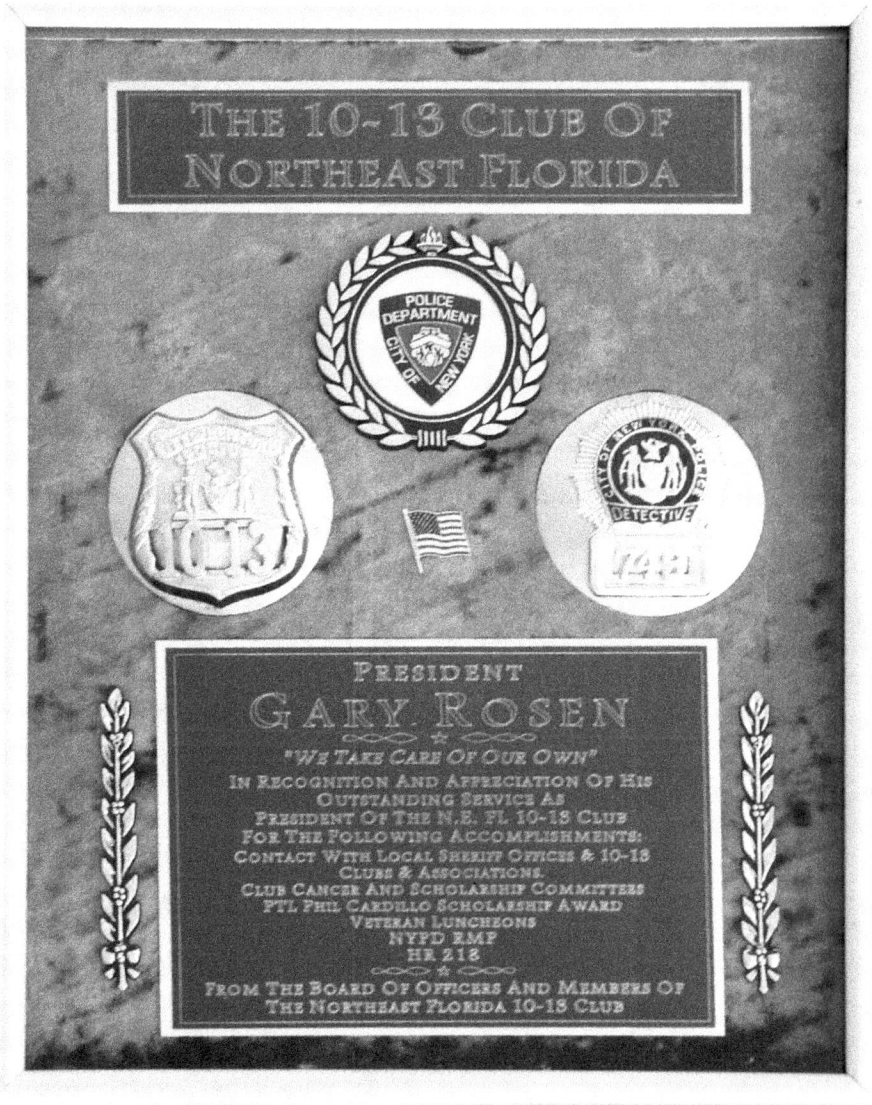

Gary Rosen
Presidential Award
for Service 2009-2011, 2014-2015
President of Northeast, FL 10-13 Club

June 14, 2021

Dear Gary,

Wow! What an incredible book! I think your book is absolutely wonderful!

I guess as a layman, I hadn't realized the emotional roller coaster a police officer goes through. The highs, the lows, the fear, the courage.

Sometimes I laughed ("uncle" chief Sidney Cooper) and sometimes I cried (PTL Phil Cardillo) but all in all your book provided me with a powerful emotional experience and a deeper perception of "the job".

Jack & I have always thought so highly of you and, as if it were'nt possible, I became even more aware of your outstanding qualities. I see your integrity, warmth, kindness, intelligence and most of all, your courage.

The love you have for your dad provided the inspiration to be the best police officer you could be. You achieved that goal + more.

There are so many things about the book that I loved. I loved the picture of you & your beautiful wife Christine. I loved the last paragraph of the ending.

Please let me know when you publish this book. I have many friends that I know will enjoy it as much as I have.

Thank you for the very kind compliment about Jack & me.

Jack & I are deeply honored to be considered your friend.

We love you.

Good luck with your book

Claire Murray

June 14, 2021

Dear Gary,

Wow! What an incredible book!. I think your book is absolutely wonderful! I guess as a layman, I hadn't realized the emotional roller coaster a police officer goes through. The highs, the lows, the fear, the courage.

Sometimes I laughed ("uncle" chief Sidney Cooper) and sometimes I cried (PTL Phil Cardillo) but all in all your book provided me with a powerful emotional experience and a deeper perception of "the job."

Jack and I have always thought so highly of you and, as if it weren't possible, I became even more aware of your outstanding qualities. I see your integrity, warmth, kindness, intelligence and most of all, your courage.

The love you have for your dad provided the inspiration to be the best police officer you could be. You achieved that goal and more. There are so many things about the book I loved. I loved the picture of you and your beautiful wife Christine. I loved the last paragraph of the ending.

Please let me know when you publish this book. I have many friends that I know will enjoy it as much as I have.

Thank you for the very kind compliment about Jack and me. Jack and I are deeply honored to be considered your friend.

We love you. Good luck with your book,

- Maria Murray

www.ingramcontent.com/pod-product-compliance
Lightning Source LLC
Chambersburg PA
CBHW062226270326
41930CB00009B/1885